Math for the Gifted Student
Challenging Activities for the Advanced Learner

Written by **Danielle Denega**

Illustrations by **John Haslam**

FlashKids

An imprint of Sterling Children's Books

FLASH KIDS, STERLING, and the distinctive Sterling logo are registered trademarks of
Sterling Publishing Co., Inc.

Published by Sterling Publishing Co., Inc.
387 Park Avenue South, New York, NY 10016
Text and illustrations © 2005 by Flash Kids
Distributed in Canada by Sterling Publishing
c/o Canadian Manda Group, 165 Dufferin Street
Toronto, Ontario, Canada M6K 3H6
Distributed in the United Kingdom by GMC Distribution Services
Castle Place, 166 High Street, Lewes, East Sussex, England BN7 1XU
Distributed in Australia by Capricorn Link (Australia) Pty. Ltd.
P.O. Box 704, Windsor, NSW 2756, Australia

Sterling ISBN 978-1-4114-3437-0

Manufactured in China

Lot #:
14 15 13
09/17

For information about custom editions, special sales, premium and
corporate purchases, please contact Sterling Special Sales
Department at 800-805-5489 or specialsales@sterlingpublishing.com.

Cover image © Tbroucek/Dreamstime.com
Cover design and production by Mada Design, Inc.

If you find that your child is unchallenged

by traditional workbooks and math practice drills, this workbook will provide the stimulation your student has been looking for. This workbook contains much more than typical fifth-grade drill pages and questions; it does not rely on the assumption that a gifted fifth grader simply requires sixth-grade work. The logic-based activities cover the national math standards for fifth grade while also providing kids with a chance to grow and challenge themselves beyond the work they do in the regular classroom. This workbook covers the curriculum areas of algebra, statistics, measurement, geometry, probability, estimation, and problem solving.

Encourage your student to use models or scrap paper to work out problems or to help him or her work through more difficult activities. Allow your student to skip around and do activities that interest him or her. The activities in the book encourage independent thinking and stimulate creativity. Your student can check his or her answers by using the answer key at the end of the book.

By utilizing this workbook series, you are providing your gifted learner an opportunity to experience scholastic achievement at an advanced level, thereby fostering confidence and an increased desire to learn.

In the Ballpark

Round the following numbers according to the instructions below.

Round to the nearest ten.

1. 8.12 _____

2. 77.34 _____

3. 469 _____

4. Circle the number line that would contain all of the numbers given.

 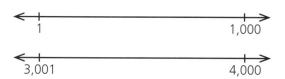

Round to the nearest hundred.

5. 231.42 _____

6. 929.24 _____

7. 4,501 _____

8. Circle the number line that would contain all of the numbers given.

 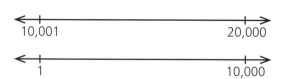

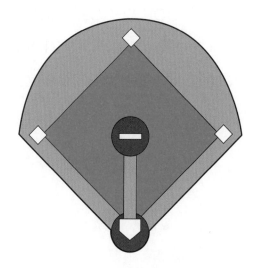

Round to the nearest thousand.

9. 8,999 _____

10. 3,456.324 _____

11. 22,524 _____

12. Circle the number line that would contain all of the numbers given.

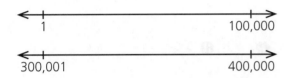 

Round to the nearest ten thousand.

13. 12,345.44 _____

14. 14,567 _____

15. 19,321 _____

16. Circle the number line that would contain all of the numbers given.

 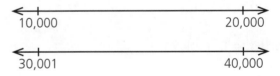

Round to the nearest hundred thousand.

17. 302,567 _____

18. 123,456.4 _____

19. 432,010 _____

20. Circle the number line that would contain all of the numbers given.

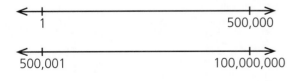 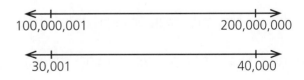

Connecting Dots

Use the diagram to solve the problems below.

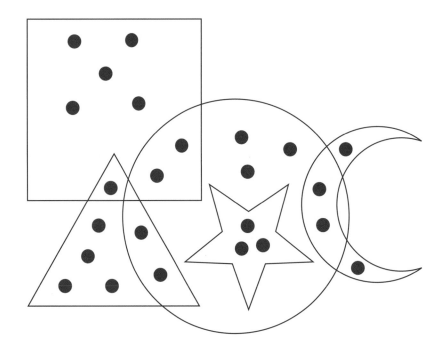

How many dots are there . . .

1. inside the square? _____

2. inside the triangle? _____

3. inside the circle? _____

4. inside the crescent? _____

5. in the intersection of the crescent and circle? _____

6. in the intersection of the square and triangle? _____

7. in the intersection of the star and circle? _____

8. in the circle, but not in any additional shapes? _____

9. in the square, but not in any additional shapes? _____

10. in the star, but not in any additional shapes? _____

Missing the Signs

Place one addition sign or subtraction sign among each series of numbers to make the statement true.
The first one has been done for you.

1. 1   2   3 **+** 7   6   5 = 888

2. 8   8   8   8   8   5   2   1 = 17,409

3. 9   4   3   2   2   1 = 722

4. 1   0   4   7   3   9   5   2   0 = 40,567

5. 7   2   2   5   7   0   0   2 = 223

6. 6   4   2   8   6   8   4   2 = 63, 444

7. 1   7   7   5   3 = 770

8. 6   3   2   3   6   7 = 2,430

9. 2   8   9   0   0   2   2   7   5   6 = 286,246

10. 8   2   6   7   3   2   1 = 8,147

Star Salaries

Use the following movie star salaries to solve the problems.

1. Melinda McMovie Star earned $2,500,000.00 for her first film. What is the place value of 5 in this salary? _____

2. For Melinda McMovie Star's tenth film, she was earning much more: $15,250,000.00! What is the place value of 1 in this salary? _____

3. If Melinda spent half of that salary on a new home, how much did her new home cost?

_____

4. Action star Franklin Famous earned $10,575,000.00 for his recent film. What is the place value of 7 in this salary? _____

5. On his next film, Franklin Famous earned an additional $3,800,500.00. What is the place value of 5 in this number? _____
How much did he earn in total for this film? _____

6. Allison Actress is the highest paid female movie star in Hollywood. She earns $25,000,000.00 per movie. What is the place value of 5 in this salary? _____

7. Before Allison Actress became famous, she worked as a waitress and earned $24,000.00 a year. What is the place value of 4 in this salary? _____
Write this salary in expanded form. _____

8. For his last film, child star Alex Actor earned three million, five hundred thousand dollars. Write this salary in standard form. _____

Forward and Backward

In language, some words read the same backward and forward. Words like this are called *palindromes*. You can make palindrome numbers, too! Just follow the steps below to make a palindrome for the numbers shown below.

1. Take 429.

2. Reverse it. You get 924.

3. Add those two numbers together.

```
  429
+ 924
 1353
```

4. Continue repeating steps 2 and 3, until you have a palindrome number!

```
  1353
+ 3531
 4884 is a palindrome!
```

Create palindromes for each number. Show your work.

1. 267

2. 624

3. 753

Goal Weight

These people are trying to shed some pounds. The fractions represent the weight they have already lost compared to their ultimate goal.

Tom $\frac{13}{26}$ Sandy $\frac{6}{24}$ Edmund $\frac{8}{56}$ Marsha $\frac{8}{10}$

Zoey $\frac{5}{25}$ Arnold $\frac{30}{45}$ Steve $\frac{5}{50}$

Reduce each person's fraction to its lowest terms.

1. Tom _____

2. Sandy _____

3. Edmund _____

4. Zoey _____

5. Arnold _____

6. Steve _____

7. Marsha _____

Now solve the problems below.

8. Which of these people has come the closest to his or her goal weight? _____

9. Which of these people is the farthest from reaching his or her goal weight? _____

10. Who is halfway to achieving his or her goal weight? _____

Building a Triangle

Pascal's triangle is a mathematical triangle developed by French mathematician Blaise Pascal. Each number in the triangle is the sum of the pair of numbers directly above it (to the above left and above right). Fill in the remaining circles to complete the Pascal's triangle below. It has been started for you.

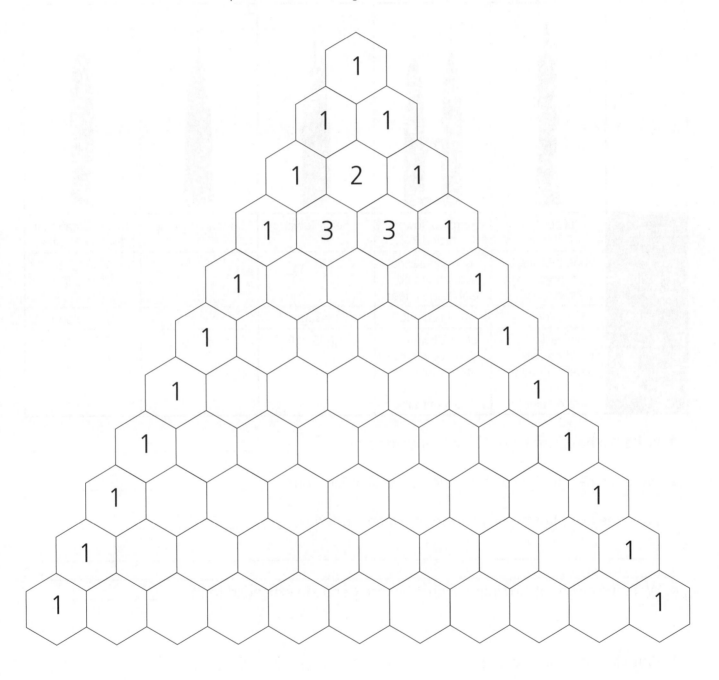

Tall Towers

The chart below shows the tallest buildings in the world, in height order.
Use the chart to answer the following questions.

Name	Taipei 101	Petronas Towers 1 and 2	Sears Tower	Jin Mao Building	Two International Finance Centre
Height	one thousand, six hundred sixty-seven feet	one thousand, four hundred eighty-three feet	1,451 feet	1,381 feet	1,362 feet
Location	Taipei	Kuala Lumpur	Chicago	Shanghai	Hong Kong
Population	two million, six hundred twenty-seven thousand, one hundred thirty-eight	one million, two hundred ninety-seven thousand, five hundred twenty-six	2,896,016	12,887,000	5,674,114

1. Write the height of Taipei 101 in standard form. _____

2. Write the height of the Petronas Towers in standard form. _____

3. Write the height of the Sears Tower in expanded form. _____

_____

4. Write the height of Two International Finance Centre in expanded form. _____

_____

5. Write the population of Taipei in standard form. _____

6. Write the population of Kuala Lumpur in standard form. _____

7. Which city has the largest population? _____

8. Round that city's population to the nearest million. _____

Product Tic-Tac-Toe

Follow the directions to play a game of tic-tac-toe. Ask a friend or a parent to play with you.

To play:

1. One player is X and the other player is O.

2. Players take turns picking one number from each column and multiplying them to find the product.

3. When the product has been determined, the player should mark that number with an X or O on the game board.

4. The first player to complete four Xs or Os in a row, a column, or a diagonal is the winner!

Column 1	Column 2
2	
3	224
5	703
7	465
9	

GAME BOARD

672	3,255	6,327	4,921
4,185	2,016	1,120	1,395
2,325	448	FREE	930
3,515	1,568	1,406	2,109

Sundae Special

Complete each division problem in the sundae glasses below. Then find the answer in the toppings bar and draw a line to its matching answer to make a sundae.

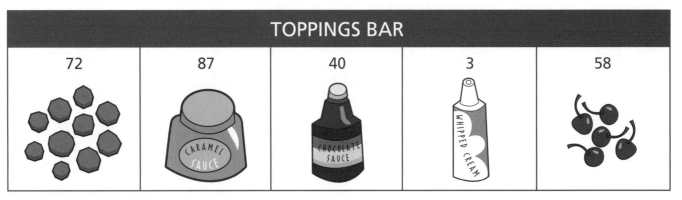

TOPPINGS BAR				
72	87	40	3	58

1. 11)792

2. 22)880

3. 31)93

4. 15)1,305

5. 79)4,582

Sale of the Season

Use the sale flyers below to solve the problems.

END-OF-SEASON SALE!

Cashmere Sweaters
Originally $109.99
40% OFF!

Peacoats
Originally $250.50
25% OFF!

Cotton Hoodies
Originally $39.99
15% OFF!

Corduroy Pants
Originally $59.50
50% OFF!

Wool socks
Originally $13.00
10% OFF!

1. What is the sale price of a pair of wool socks? _____

2. Which sale flyer shows a discount of $\frac{1}{2}$? _____

3. Which sale flyer shows a discount of $\frac{1}{4}$? _____

4. What is the sale price of a cashmere sweater? _____

5. What is the sale price of a pair of corduroy pants? _____

6. Which sale flyer shows a discount of $\frac{1}{10}$? _____

7. Which sale flyer shows a discount of $\frac{2}{5}$? _____

8. Which sale flyer shows a discount of $\frac{3}{20}$? _____

9. What is the sale price of a cotton hoodie? _____

10. Which sale flyer shows a discount of $\frac{3}{12}$? _____

Weathering Integers

We use integers in everyday life when we talk about the weather.
Use the weather forecast to solve the problems that follow.

Monday	Tuesday	Wednesday	Thursday	Friday	Saturday	Sunday
High 25°F Low 16°F	**High 18°F** Low 6°F	**High 2°F** Low –8°F	**High 5°F** Low 0°F	**High 3°F** Low –4°F	**High 12°F** Low –1°F	**High 29°F** Low 19°F
Chance of snow showers	Partly cloudy	Cloudy	Sunny	Partly cloudy	Cloudy	Snow showers

1. Shade in the week's highest predicted temperature on the thermometer.

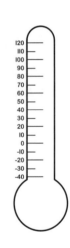

2. What is the absolute value of the integer represented by this temperature? _____

3. What is the opposite of the integer represented by this temperature? _____

4. Shade in the week's lowest predicted temperature on the thermometer.

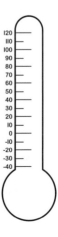

5. What is the absolute value of the integer represented by this temperature? _____

6. What is the opposite of the integer represented by this temperature? _____

7. What is the difference between the predicted high and low temperatures on Monday?

_____

8. What is the difference between the predicted high and low temperatures on Wednesday?

_____

9. Cold front! Saturday's predicted temperatures each fall 15 degrees. What are they now?

_____

10. Warm front! Thursday's predicted temperatures each rise 11 degrees. What are they now?

_____

11. Shade in the mean predicted high temperature for the week.
Round your answer to the nearest whole degree.

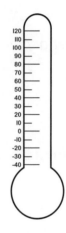

12. What is the absolute value of the mean predicted high temperature for the week? _____

13. Shade in the mean predicted low temperature for the week.
Round your answer to the nearest whole degree.

14. What is the absolute value of the mean predicted low temperature for the week? _____

Ball Pit

Use the picture below to solve the problems.

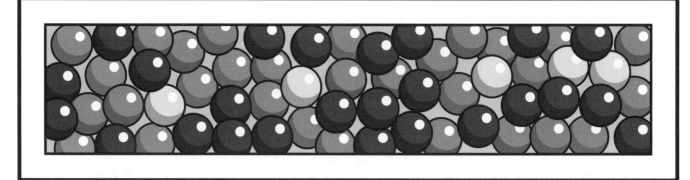

1. Write the number of blue balls as a fraction in lowest terms. _____

2. Write the number of orange balls as a fraction in lowest terms. _____

3. Write the number of red balls as a fraction in lowest terms. _____

4. Write the number of green balls as a fraction in lowest terms. _____

5. Write the number of yellow balls as a fraction in lowest terms. _____

6. What is the ratio of blue balls to green balls? _____

7. What is the ratio of red balls to the whole? _____

8. What is the ratio of orange balls to yellow balls? _____

9. Which is greater: the number of red balls or the number of yellow balls? Write their relationship in numbers. _____

10. Which is greater: the number of green balls or the number of orange balls? Write their relationship in numbers. _____

Market Watch

Put the following stock values in ascending order.

1.

ARP	DELL	QUIQ	ZOE	DBB
0.016	0.13	1.36	0.1	0.136

_____   _____   _____   _____   _____

2.

EAO	VOX	CAD	BOX	SAW
0.123	0.132	1.23	0.03	0.30

_____   _____   _____   _____   _____

3.

HIG	CLE	NEW	COM	KAT
0.6	0.08	0.65	0.12	0.51

_____   _____   _____   _____   _____

Put the following stock values in descending order.

4.

CRYS	MOT	OSL	BEL	HAR
3.49	3.56	4.0	3.546	4.02

_____   _____   _____   _____   _____

5.

AUW	JUL	MAR	JAN	OCTI
100.9	101.0	106.25	101.04	10.10

_____   _____   _____   _____   _____

6.

ESP	KEG	SLU	GEB	KTT
1.88	1.95	1.59	1.31	1.80

_____   _____   _____   _____   _____

The market has crashed! Use the stock information above to determine the new values of the stocks listed.

7. The value of BEL decreases by 0.43 points. _____

8. The value of CAD decreases by 1.1 points. _____

Homework Help

Howard needs homework help! Help him by finishing the prime factorization trees he's not completed yet. If a tree is complete as it is, write *complete* below it.

1. 15
/ \
3   5

_____

2. 42
/ \
7   6

_____

3. 55
/ \
11   5

_____

4. 24
/ \
4   6
/ \
2   2

_____

5. 30
/ \
5   6

_____

6. 56
/ \
7   8
/ \
4   2

_____

7. 63
/ \
9   7

_____

8. 21
/ \
3   7

_____

9. 90
/ \
9   10
/ \
3   3

_____

Piles of Homework

The numbers below reflect how many hours each student has spent on his or her homework this week. Draw a line to match each improper fraction to its mixed or whole number in its simplest form.

1. Ben $\dfrac{23}{8}$ $2\dfrac{3}{4}$

2. Jennifer $\dfrac{27}{8}$ $1\dfrac{4}{5}$

3. Margaret $\dfrac{25}{6}$ $2\dfrac{7}{8}$

4. Courtney $\dfrac{11}{4}$ $3\dfrac{3}{8}$

5. Jesse $\dfrac{9}{5}$ $4\dfrac{1}{6}$

Rewrite each mixed number as an improper fraction.

6. Malcolm $3\dfrac{7}{8}$ _____

7. Jake $4\dfrac{1}{5}$ _____

8. Susie $3\dfrac{1}{10}$ _____

9. Which student spent the most time on his or her homework this week? _____

     Which student spent the least time on his or her homework this week? _____

10. What is the difference in time spent by the two students in question 9? Write your answer as both a fraction and a mixed number. _____

In the Doghouse

Look at each dog's score in the dog show. Some did very well and some did very poorly. Use the scores to answer the questions.

dalmation 7

poodle –11

shih Tzu –4

pug 12

foxhound 10

terrier 5

Labrador retriever –9

rottweiler 3

golden retriever –2

1. Put the dogs' scores in order from smallest to largest. Use their breed names.

_____   _____   _____

_____   _____   _____

_____   _____   _____

2. How many dogs have scores greater than the rottweiler's score? _____

3. How many dogs have scores greater than the pug's score? _____

4. How many dogs have scores less than the golden retriever's score? _____

5. How many dogs have scores less than the terrier's score? _____

Now, compare the scores by writing **<**, **>**, or **=**.

6. poodle _____ pug

7. golden retriever _____ shih tzu

8. foxhound _____ dalmation

9. rottweiler _____ pug

10. shih tzu _____ Labrador retriever

Now, solve these addition and subtraction problems using each dog's score.

11. terrier + poodle = _____

12. shih tzu + pug = _____

13. dalmation − foxhound = _____

14. golden retriever − Labrador retriever = _____

15. terrier + foxhound + pug = _____

16. shih tzu + golden retriever + poodle = _____

17. foxhound − terrier − rottweiler = _____

18. dalmation − pug + terrier = _____

19. rottweiler − pug + poodle = _____

20. Labrador retriever − rottweiler + poodle + dalmation = _____

Decimal Pyramids

Help build the decimal pyramids. Start at the bottom of each pyramid. Each set of numbers that sit side-by-side equal the one above them when added. Using this information, fill in the empty blocks in each pyramid.

1.

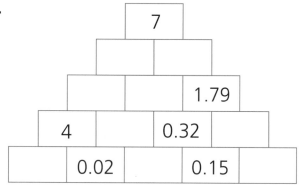

2.

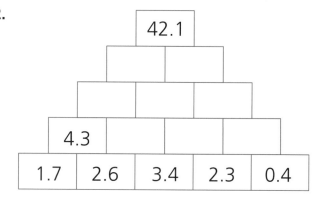

3.

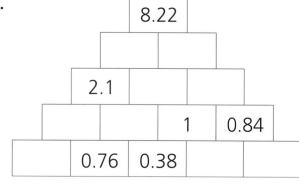

4.

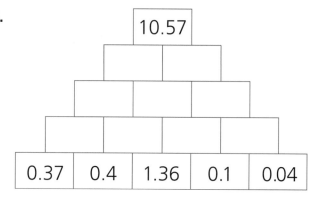

5.

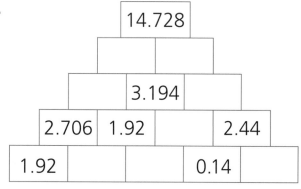

6.

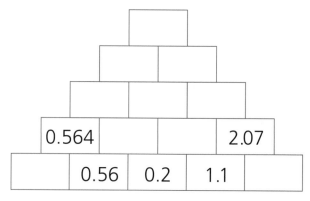

24

Video Game Mania

Video games have gotten expensive. Use the sale flyers to solve the problems below.

SUPERBUG!
Only **$49.00**

POP BAND
$59.00

BASEBALL
ALL STARS 2009
Now just **$63.00**

ROCK STAR
2009 Edition
$62.00

TOTAL ENFORCEMENT
This week only!
$39.99

BASEBALL
ALL STARS 2008
Just reduced to **$40.00**

MILITARY MAN
Just reduced to **$59.99**

1. List the games from most expensive to least expensive.

_____   _____

_____   _____

_____   _____

_____

2. Which would cost more, three Pop Bands or two Baseball All Stars 2009? What is the difference in price? _____

3. Which is less expensive, two Superbug! games or one Military Man game? What is the difference in price? _____

4. Adam received $50.00 to spend on a video game. List the individual games he could get without going over budget. _____

_____   _____

5. Before Baseball All Stars 2008 was reduced to its current sale price, it cost $50.00. How much has the price been reduced? _____ The price reduction is _____%.

What Time Is It?

Record in numerals the time shown on each clock.

1.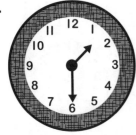

_____

2.

_____

3.

_____

4. If all of the clocks above are showing PM time, which clock shows the latest time? _____

5. If all of the clocks above are showing AM time, which clock shows the earliest time? _____

Draw hands on each clock to show the time indicated.

6. Quarter past four

Now, draw the time if one hour and forty minutes have passed.

7. Ten minutes to seven

Now, draw the time if three hours and fifteen minutes have passed.

8. Half past nine

Now, draw the time if twenty-five minutes have passed.

To the Letter

Use the picture below to solve the problems.

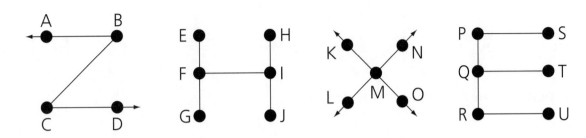

1. Name five points. _____ _____ _____ _____ _____

2. Name two lines. _____ _____

3. Name two rays. _____ _____

4. Name five line segments. _____ _____ _____ _____ _____

5. Name a pair of parallel line segments. _____ _____

6. What is another letter of the alphabet that contains parallel lines? Draw it here. Create points, like the ones in the examples above. Then, indicate which lines are parallel.

7. Name a pair of perpendicular line segments. _____ _____

8. What is another letter of the alphabet that contains perpendicular lines? Draw it here. Create points, like the ones in the examples above. Then, indicate which lines are perpendicular.

On the Line

Use the number line to solve the problems below.

```
A    B    C    D    E    F    G    H    I    J    K    L    M    N    O    P    Q    R    S    T    U
├────┼────┼────┼────┼────┼────┼────┼────┼────┼────┼────┼────┼────┼────┼────┼────┼────┼────┼────┼────┤
-5  -4.5  -4  -3.5  -3  -2.5  -2  -1.5  -1  -0.5  0   0.5   1   1.5   2   2.5   3   3.5   4   4.5   5
```

1. Which point on the number line *best* represents −4? _____

2. Which point on the number line *best* represents 1.5? _____

3. Which point on the number line *best* represents 2.55? _____

4. Which point on the number line *best* represents −4.9? _____

5. Which point on the number line *best* represents 0? _____

6. Which point on the number line *best* represents −3.9? _____

7. Which point on the number line *best* represents 1.4? _____

8. Which point on the number line *best* represents 3.1? _____

9. Which point on the number line *best* represents −2.06? _____

10. Which point on the number line *best* represents 2? _____

Sports Arenas

Determine the perimeter of the following sports arenas. Use the information in the box to help you.

> Rectangle: Perimeter = 2(*l* + *w*)   Triangle: Perimeter = *s* + *s* + *s*
>
> Circle: Perimeter = πd Other Polygons: Perimeter = sum of sides
>
> Square: Perimeter = 4*s*

1. Tennis court

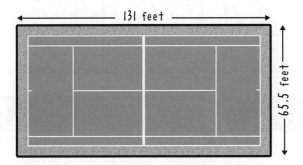

131 feet

65.5 feet

_____

2. Softball field

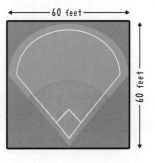

60 feet

60 feet

_____

3. Soccer field

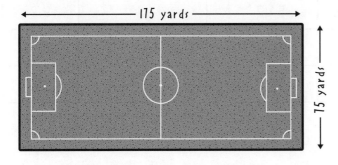

175 yards

75 yards

_____

4. Wrestling ring

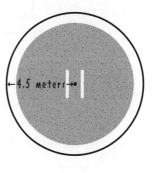

4.5 meters

_____

5. L-shaped pool

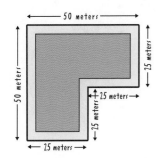

50 meters

25 meters

50 meters

25 meters

25 meters

25 meters

_____

Track Meet

At the track and field world championships, athletes came through with strong results.
Use the results boards to solve the problems below.

Women's 100-Meter Dash	
France	11.35
United States	10.49
Germany	11.09
Hungary	10.73

Women's 800-Meter Race	
Ukraine	2:02.64
France	2:01.55
Kenya	2:02.59
Great Britain	2:02.61
Germany	2:02.73

Women's High Jump	
Russia	2.01
Sweden	2.00
Poland	2.09
Bulgaria	2.08
Ukraine	1.92

Men's 400-Meter Hurdles	
Germany	48.27
France	47.37
United States	46.78

Men's Pole Vault	
Germany	5.52
Czech Republic	5.02
Poland	5.52
Czech Republic	5.42
Germany	5.62
Great Britain	5.22

Men's Shot Put	
Czech Republic	18.14
Russia	19.75
Latvia	19.44
Germany	19.22
Ukraine	19.52
Slovakia	18.64

1. Put the Men's Shot Put results in descending order, by country.

_____

_____

_____

_____

_____

2. Put the Women's 100-Meter Dash results in ascending order, by country.

_____

_____

_____

_____

3. Put the Women's 800-Meter Race results in descending order, by country.

_____

_____

_____

_____

_____

4. In high jump, the longest jump wins. Who won the women's high jump? _____

5. In races, the fastest, or lowest time, wins the race. Who won the Men's 400-Meter Hurdles?

_____

6. In pole vault, the highest vault wins. Who won the Men's Pole Vault? _____

7. Which country won the most events? _____

8. Which country placed in the most events? _____

9. If there are 3.28 feet in one meter, how many feet is an 800-meter race? _____

How many feet is a 100-meter race? _____

How many feet is a 400-meter race? _____

10. What is the mean of the Men's Pole Vault results? Round your answer to the nearest hundredth.

_____

Averaging Out

Find three friends or family members and record all of the following information for them and for yourself. Then solve the problems below.

First Name	Number of Letters in First Name	Number of Letters in Last Name	Height in Inches	Age in Months
1.				
2.				
3.				
4.				
Total				
Average				

1. Whose first name has the number of letters closest to the average? _____

2. Whose last name has the number of letters closest to the average? _____

3. Whose height is closest to the average? _____

4. Whose age is closest to the average? _____

Finding Numbers

Read the numbers written in expanded form, then find and circle them in standard form in the number puzzle. They may be written horizontally or vertically, and they may overlap.

8	5	3	7	6	5	4	9	0
5	1	0	2	7	4	8	6	1
1	3	5	7	9	2	4	6	8
2	4	6	8	0	1	3	5	7
9	7	4	2	1	3	5	0	7
6	3	8	0	1	5	3	8	5
0	8	6	5	2	4	3	6	4
8	0	2	5	0	8	1	5	3
2	4	8	4	2	6	5	0	1
7	9	3	9	2	9	5	1	4

1. Sixty-five thousand, four hundred ninety

2. Six million, four hundred eighty-six thousand, two hundred eighty-three

3. Eight million, twenty-five thousand, eighty-one

4. Fifty-four thousand, two hundred thirteen

5. Two hundred ninety-six thousand, eighty-two

6. Five thousand, one hundred two

7. One thousand, three hundred forty-seven

8. Six million, eight hundred one thousand, three hundred fifty-seven

9. Ninety-three million, nine hundred twenty-nine thousand, five hundred fourteen

10. One hundred eighty-seven thousand, seven hundred fifty-four

Where in the World?

Use the map to answer the questions below.

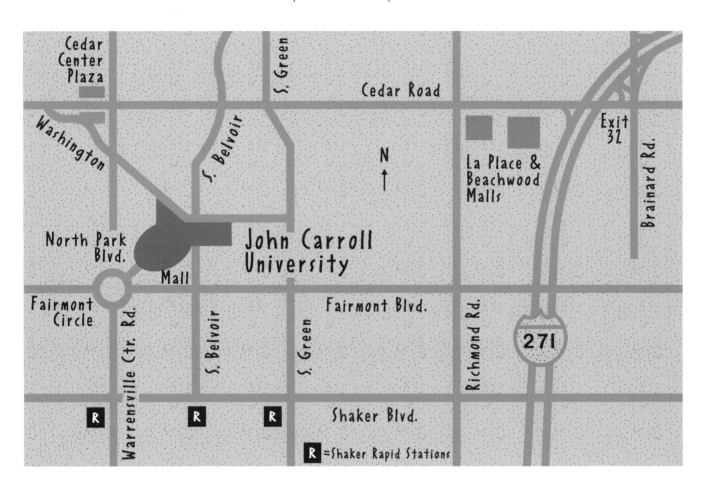

1. *True* or *False*? Fairmont Boulevard is perpendicular to Shaker Boulevard. _____

2. *True* or *False*? South Belvoir Street is parallel to South Green Street. _____

3. *True* or *False*? Richmond Road is perpendicular to Fairmont Boulevard. _____

4. *True* or *False*? Cedar Road is parallel to Richmond Road. _____

5. *True* or *False*? Warrensville Center Road intersects Richmond Road. _____

6. You are at the intersection of Cedar Road and North Park Boulevard. Where are you?

_____

7. You are at the intersection of Cedar Road and Richmond Road. Where are you?

_____

8. A friend needs to get from Fairmont Circle to La Place & Beechwood Malls. Write directions for your friend.

_____

_____

_____

_____

Weather System

Use the information on the thermometers to solve the problems.

1. Record the temperature shown on the thermometer.

_____

The temperature decreases 12 degrees. Shade in the thermometer to show the temperature change.

Add these two integers using their absolute values. What is their sum? _____

2. Record the temperature shown on the thermometer.

_____

The temperature increases 23 degrees. Shade in the thermometer to show the temperature change.

Add these two integers using their absolute values. What is their sum? _____

3. Record the temperature shown on the thermometer.

_____

The temperature increases four degrees. Shade in the thermometer to show the temperature change.

Add these two integers using their absolute values. What is their sum? _____

Clothing Catalog

Use the clothing catalog to solve the problems.

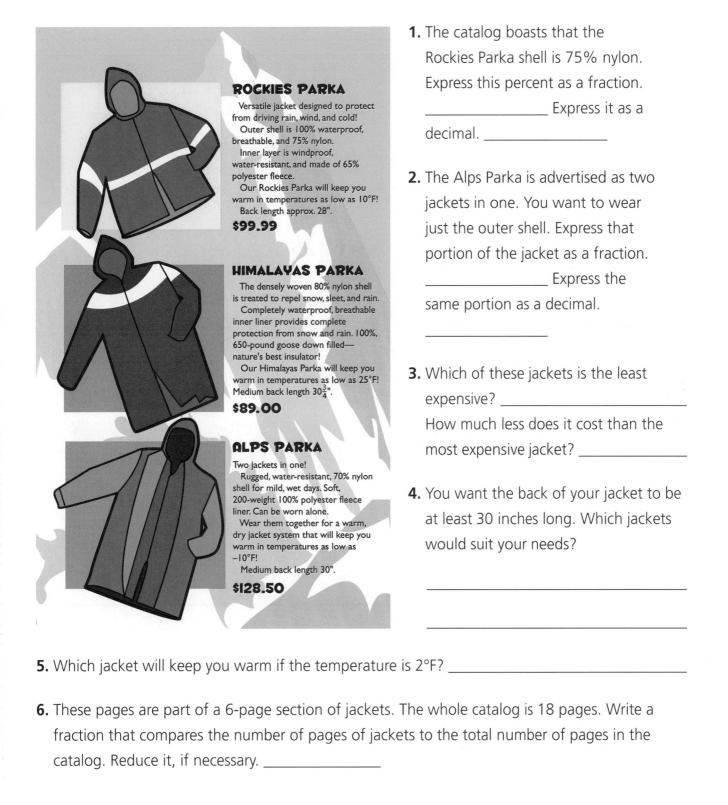

ROCKIES PARKA

Versatile jacket designed to protect from driving rain, wind, and cold!
Outer shell is 100% waterproof, breathable, and 75% nylon.
Inner layer is windproof, water-resistant, and made of 65% polyester fleece.
Our Rockies Parka will keep you warm in temperatures as low as 10°F! Back length approx. 28".

$99.99

HIMALAYAS PARKA

The densely woven 80% nylon shell is treated to repel snow, sleet, and rain.
Completely waterproof, breathable inner liner provides complete protection from snow and rain. 100%, 650-pound goose down filled—nature's best insulator!
Our Himalayas Parka will keep you warm in temperatures as low as 25°F! Medium back length $30\frac{3}{4}$".

$89.00

ALPS PARKA

Two jackets in one!
Rugged, water-resistant, 70% nylon shell for mild, wet days. Soft, 200-weight 100% polyester fleece liner. Can be worn alone.
Wear them together for a warm, dry jacket system that will keep you warm in temperatures as low as −10°F!
Medium back length 30".

$128.50

1. The catalog boasts that the Rockies Parka shell is 75% nylon. Express this percent as a fraction. _____ Express it as a decimal. _____

2. The Alps Parka is advertised as two jackets in one. You want to wear just the outer shell. Express that portion of the jacket as a fraction. _____ Express the same portion as a decimal. _____

3. Which of these jackets is the least expensive? _____ How much less does it cost than the most expensive jacket? _____

4. You want the back of your jacket to be at least 30 inches long. Which jackets would suit your needs?

_____

_____

5. Which jacket will keep you warm if the temperature is 2°F? _____

6. These pages are part of a 6-page section of jackets. The whole catalog is 18 pages. Write a fraction that compares the number of pages of jackets to the total number of pages in the catalog. Reduce it, if necessary. _____

Cold Snap

The integers below represent temperatures. Put them in order from coldest to warmest.

1. 20, 4, –4, 18, 8   _____ _____ _____ _____ _____

2. 32, –32, 30, –30, 3   _____ _____ _____ _____ _____

3. 0, 1, –1, –3, 10   _____ _____ _____ _____ _____

4. 6, 9, –6, 0, 5   _____ _____ _____ _____ _____

Now compare the two temperatures using **<**, **>**, or **=**. Then, write the absolute value of the greater integer.

5. –4 _____ –8

Absolute value of the greater integer: _____

6. –6 _____ –11

Absolute value of the greater integer: _____

7. 0 _____ 5

Absolute value of the greater integer: _____

8. 3 _____ –3

Absolute value of the greater integer: _____

High Dive

For each dive shown, indicate whether the angle formed by the diver's body is *acute*, *obtuse*, or *right*. Then, using a protractor, measure and record each angle.

1.

Is this an acute, obtuse, or right angle? _____

How many degrees does the angle measure? _____

2.

Is this an acute, obtuse, or right angle? _____

How many degrees does the angle measure? _____

3.

Is this an acute, obtuse, or right angle? _____

How many degrees does the angle measure? _____

4.

Is this an acute, obtuse, or right angle? _____

How many degrees does the angle measure? _____

5.

Is this an acute, obtuse, or right angle? _____

How many degrees does the angle measure? _____

The Shape of Things

Solve the problems using the flags of the world shown below.

1. Shade in the trapezoids. Name one other shape in this flag.

_____

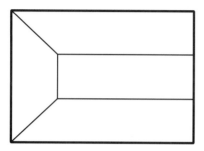

2. Shade in the parallelogram. Name one other shape in this flag.

_____

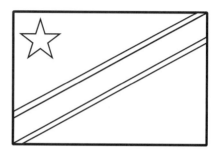

3. Shade in the pentagon. Name one other shape in this flag.

_____

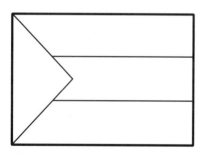

4. Shade in the quadrilaterals. Name one other shape in this flag.

_____

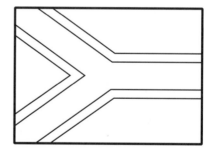

5. Shade in the rhombus. Name one other shape in this flag.

_____

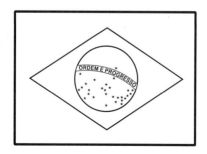

6. Shade in the stars. Name one other shape in this flag.

_____

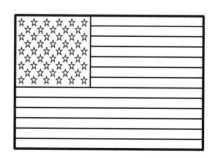

Pascal's Secrets

Shade in each of the odd numbers in the Pascal's triangle below.

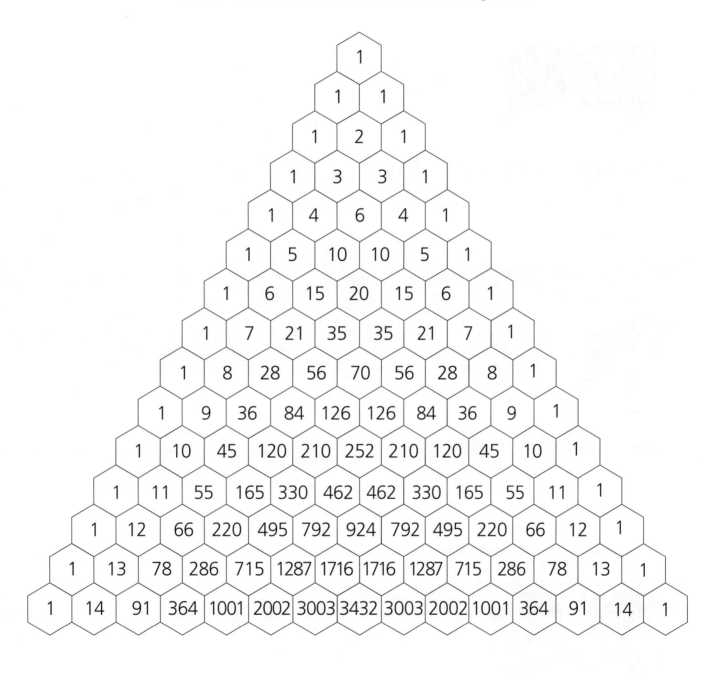

1. What larger shapes are revealed to you? _____

2. How many of these shapes are unshaded? _____

3. How many of these shapes are there *in total* in the image? _____

Table Trouble

Use the tables of varying shapes to solve the problems.

1.

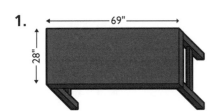

What is the area (in square inches) of the table? _____

The tablecloth for this table is 12 inches wider than the table on each side. What are its dimensions? _____

What is the perimeter of the tablecloth? _____

2.

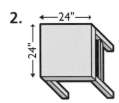

What is the area (in square inches) of the table? _____

The tablecloth for this table is 10 inches wider than the table on each side. What are its dimensions? _____

What is the perimeter of the tablecloth? _____

3.

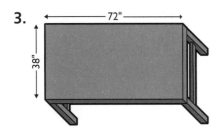

What is the area (in square inches) of the table? _____

The tablecloth for this table is 14 inches wider than the table on each side. What are its dimensions? _____

What is the perimeter of the tablecloth? _____

Prime Factorization

Determine the prime factors of the numbers below. Show your work.

1. 60 factored into prime numbers is:

_____

2. 45 factored into prime numbers is:

_____

3. 20 factored into prime numbers is:

_____

4. 66 factored into prime numbers is:

_____

5. 25 factored into prime numbers is:

_____

6. 64 factored into prime numbers is:

_____

7. 32 factored into prime numbers is:

_____

8. 24 factored into prime numbers is:

_____

9. 81 factored into prime numbers is:

_____

10. 10 factored into prime numbers is:

_____

11. 96 factored into prime numbers is:

_____

12. 84 factored into prime numbers is:

_____

Secret Message

Fill in the missing numbers to complete the patterns.

1. 22   24   _____   28

2. 12   _____   18   21

3. _____   12   4   –4

4. 11   5   _____   –7

5. 30   22   14   _____

6. 24   16   _____   0

7. 17   41   65   _____

8. 14   _____   64   89

9. _____   100   1,000   10,000

10. 56   _____   14   7

Now use the key to reveal a secret message! In order of the answers above, write the letter or symbol that corresponds with the answer.

A = 15	H = –1	O = 54	V = 4
B = –2	I = 80	P = 0	W = 60
C = 77	J = 22	Q = 34	X = 49
D = 41	K = –7	R = 6	Y = 19
E = 39	L = 89	S = 10	Z = –14
F = 30	M = 26	T = 20	? = 50
G = 93	N = 65	U = 8	! = 28

SECRET CODE

___ ___ ___ ___   ___ ___ ___ ___ ___

Time for Television

The problems below are missing something. Can you tell what?
Give the information you would need to solve the problem.

1. Sam holds the world record for consecutive hours watching television. How many more hours did he log than his closest competitor? _____

_____

2. *Grey's Emergency* has won 17 Emmy Awards. How many of these did the show win prior to 2009? _____

_____

3. Meghan watches television for three hours per day. How does this compare to the national average? _____

_____

4. The television is 42 inches wide and 25 inches high. The cabinet it needs to go into is 48 inches wide. Will the television fit inside the cabinet? _____

_____

5. The ratings for *Desperate Actresses* have been very high. It was the most watched show for three of the past four weeks. What was its ranking for that other week? _____

_____

6. The Smiths are shopping for a new television set. The 37-inch one costs $999.99. The 42-inch version originally cost $1,300.00 but is on sale this week. Which television costs less? _____

_____

Table Triangle Art

Using the key, write the number that corresponds with the shape on the mosaic table.

Key

1 Right Triangles

2 Scalene Triangles

3 Equilateral Triangles

4 Isosceles Triangles

5 Other Shapes

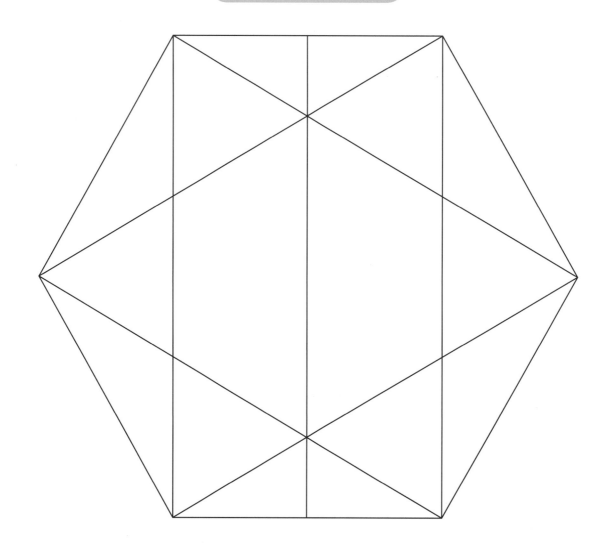

Shelter Facts

Circle the piece or pieces of information that will allow you to solve each problem. Then answer each question.

1. Problem: How many cats came to the shelter in a week?

   a. Monday through Friday, 12 cats came into the shelter.

   b. The shelter feeds cats $2\frac{1}{2}$ cups of food per day.

   c. On Saturday and Sunday, 4 cats came into the shelter.

   Answer: _____

2. Problem: What percentage of dogs at the shelter are mixed breeds?

   a. There are 3 collies at the shelter.

   b. 2 of the dogs at the shelter are cockapoos.

   c. Of the 50 dogs at the shelter, 20 are purebred.

   Answer: _____

3. Problem: How many square feet get mopped each day?

   a. The dog area is 90' × 50'.

   b. The dog area is mopped once in the morning and once in the evening.

   c. Of the dog area, 2,000 square feet is outdoors and does not get mopped.

   Answer: _____

4. Problem: How many weeks will it take for a dog blanket to shrink by 12%?

   a. The dog blankets get washed 3 times per week.

   b. There are 105 dog blankets.

   c. The blankets shrink 0.8% after each washing.

   Answer: _____

5. Problem: How many hours did the kitten sleep Sunday through Wednesday?

   a. The kitten slept for $8\frac{1}{2}$ hours on Sunday night.

   b. On Monday, Tuesday, and Wednesday nights, the kitten slept for 7 hours per night.

   c. The kitten slept for $9\frac{1}{4}$ hours on Friday night.

   Answer: _____

47

What's Cooking?

Use the information in the recipes to solve each problem.

Macaroni and Cheese

Serves 6

5 tablespoons butter

3 tablespoons flour

$2\frac{1}{2}$ cups milk

1 lb cheddar cheese

$\frac{1}{2}$ lb Colby cheese

1 tablespoon Dijon mustard

$\frac{1}{8}$ teaspoon nutmeg

$\frac{1}{8}$ teaspoon cayenne pepper

$\frac{1}{4}$ teaspoon each salt and pepper

1 pound elbow macaroni

$\frac{3}{4}$ cup bread crumbs

1. Rewrite this recipe to serve 12 people.

_____   _____

_____   _____

_____   _____

_____   _____

_____   _____

_____

2. Rewrite this recipe to serve 3 people.

_____   _____

_____   _____

_____   _____

_____   _____

_____

Bean and Beef Chili

Serves 8

2 onions	1 tablespoon cumin
3 garlic cloves	1 teaspoon oregano
1 lb lean ground beef	1 teaspoon coriander
2 cups diced tomatoes	1 teaspoon salt
$1\frac{1}{2}$ cups tomato paste	7 ounces black beans
1 cup beef broth	4 chili peppers

3. Rewrite this recipe to serve 2 people.

_____   _____

_____   _____

_____   _____

_____   _____

_____   _____

4. Rewrite this recipe to serve 24 people.

_____   _____

_____   _____

_____   _____

_____   _____

_____   _____

Candy Counter

At the candy counter, candy is measured by the pound. Use the price list to solve the problems below. Round monetary answers to the nearest cent.

GUMMY CHEWS	**$0.49 lb**
LICORICE TWISTS	**$0.75 lb**
CHOCOLATE KISSES	**$1.25 lb**
CHOCOLATE PEANUT-BUTTER HEARTS	**$1.09 lb**
MALT BALLS	**$0.89 lb**
PEPPERMINT PATTIES	**$1.35 lb**

1. How much will it cost to purchase $\frac{1}{2}$ pound of chocolate peanut-butter hearts? _____

2. How much will it cost to purchase $1\frac{1}{2}$ pounds of malt balls? _____

3. How much will it cost to purchase $\frac{1}{4}$ pound of gummy chews? _____

4. How much will it cost to purchase $\frac{3}{4}$ pound of peppermint patties? _____

5. How much will it cost to purchase $2\frac{1}{4}$ pounds of licorice twists? _____

6. You purchase 2 pounds of peppermint patties, but you save $0.40 by using a store coupon. How much have you saved per pound of candy? _____

It's a candy shopping spree! In 30 seconds, you are able to grab the following:

7. $2.18 worth of chocolate peanut-butter hearts. How many pounds is this? _____

8. $2.45 worth of gummy chews. How many pounds is this? _____

9. $3.50 worth of chocolate kisses. How many pounds is this? _____

10. $2.67 worth of malt balls. How many pounds is this? _____

Population Estimation

The numbers below represent the population in different cities. Round the populations to the nearest hundred thousand.

1. 899,412 _____

2. 100,353 _____

3. 648,205 _____

4. Which of these populations do you think is closest to the population of Green Bay, Wisconsin, one of the smaller cities in the country? _____

Round the populations to the nearest million.

5. 1,056,789 _____

6. 4,143,734 _____

7. 8,250,823 _____

8. Which of these populations do you think is closest to the population of New York City, the largest city in the country? _____

Round the populations to the nearest billion.

9. 2,692,012,826 _____

10. 1,012,987,429 _____

11. 6,707,590,132 _____

12. Which of these populations do you think is closest to the population of earth?

_____

Cafeteria Crunch

The graph shows the total number of lunches purchased in the cafeteria each year over a period of years.
Use the graph to solve the problems.

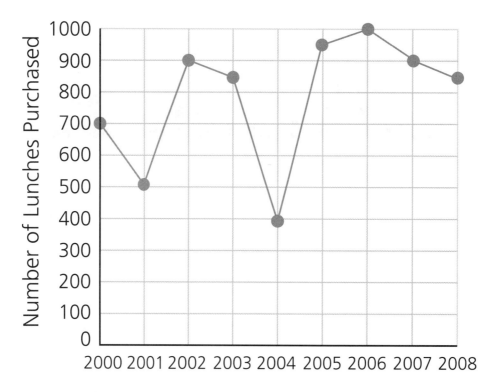

1. What information appears on the x-axis? _____

2. What information appears on the y-axis? _____

3. In what year were the most lunches purchased? _____

4. In what year were the fewest lunches purchased? _____

Circle the best answer.

5. The greatest increase in the number of lunches purchased occurred between which two years?

    a. 2001 and 2002

    b. 2004 and 2005

    c. 2005 and 2006

    d. 2007 and 2008

6. The greatest decrease in the number of lunches purchased occurred between which two years?

    a. 2000 and 2001

    b. 2006 and 2007

    c. 2007 and 2008

    d. 2003 and 2004

The Time It Takes

The map below outlines how long it takes to walk to each location from home.
Use the map to solve the problems. Reduce all fractions to lowest terms.

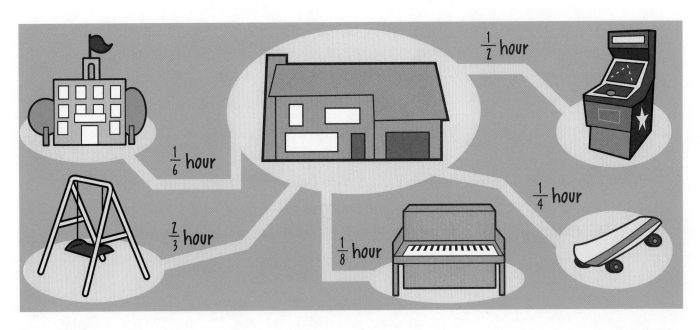

1. How long would it take to walk to school and home again? _____

How many minutes is this? _____

2. How long would it take to walk to the skate park and home again? _____

How many minutes is this? _____

3. How long would it take to walk to the playground and home again, and then to the arcade?

_____ How many minutes is this? _____

4. How long would it take to walk to piano lessons and home again, then to the playground?

_____ How many minutes is this? _____

5. How long would it take to walk halfway to the arcade, and then home again? _____

How many minutes is this? _____

In the Big Apple

Word problems sometimes offer more information than is necessary to answer the question. For each problem below, underline the portions that provide too much information. Then solve the problem.

1. Marcus drove 645 miles to get to New York City, where he spent four nights at a hotel that cost $199.00 per night. While in New York, Marcus walked to all the tourist destinations, a total of 46 miles altogether. How many fewer miles did Marcus walk than he drove in the car? _____

2. Each member of a 52-member New York City Police Department precinct has three different uniforms that consist of two pieces each. The uniforms cost $75.00 each, plus tax. When the precinct launders all of their uniforms, how many pieces of clothing get washed? _____

3. The 5K run in Central Park had 800 runners competing. Of the runners, 1.5% did not finish the 5K. Of the runners that finished, 369 were male. The winner was a surprising 58 years old, while the average age of all the runners was only 32. How many women finished the race? _____

4. Even though Jane lives in New York City and walks about 4 miles per day, she still wears high-heeled shoes all the time. Her favorite brand of shoes costs $150 per pair, and she buys four new pairs per year. How much has Jane spent on shoes in the past three years? _____

5. After work today, Sam and his 23 colleagues ate 12 pizzas, 6 of which were anchovy, 4 of which were plain cheese, and 2 of which had mushrooms and peppers. Each pizza had 8 slices. How many slices did each person eat if they all ate the same amount? _____

Thinking Inside the Box

Using all of the numbers listed for each problem, fill in the blank boxes to make a fraction that results in a true statement.

1. Use 1, 2, 3, 4

$$\frac{\square}{\square} + \frac{\square}{\square} = \frac{5}{4}$$

2. Use 1, 3, 5, 10

$$\frac{\square}{\square} + \frac{\square}{\square} = \frac{7}{10}$$

3. Use 1, 1, 2, 3

$$\frac{\square}{\square} + \frac{\square}{\square} = \frac{5}{6}$$

4. Use 1, 1, 3, 5

$$\frac{\square}{\square} + \frac{\square}{\square} = \frac{8}{15}$$

5. Use 1, 2, 3, 5

$$\frac{\square}{\square} - \frac{\square}{\square} = \frac{7}{15}$$

6. Use 3, 7, 8, 8

$$\frac{\square}{\square} - \frac{\square}{\square} = \frac{1}{2}$$

7. Use 1, 3, 3, 4

$$\frac{\square}{\square} - \frac{\square}{\square} = \frac{5}{12}$$

8. Use 1, 1, 2, 6

$$\frac{\square}{\square} - \frac{\square}{\square} = \frac{1}{3}$$

Factoring with Pascal's Triangle

Follow the directions below to complete each Pascal's triangle.

1. Shade in the numbers that are divisible by 2.

2. Circle the numbers that are divisible by 3.

3. Shade in the prime numbers.

4. Circle the composite numbers.

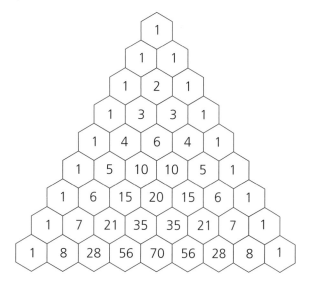

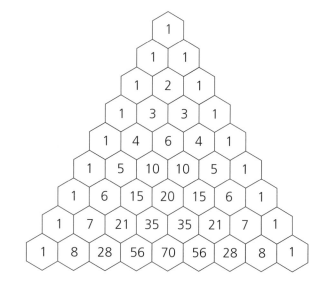

5. Shade in the numbers divisible by 7.

6. Circle the numbers divisible by 10.

7. Shade in the numbers divisible by 4.

8. Circle the numbers divisible by 5.

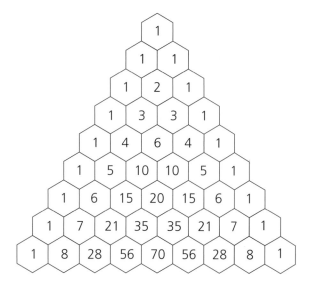

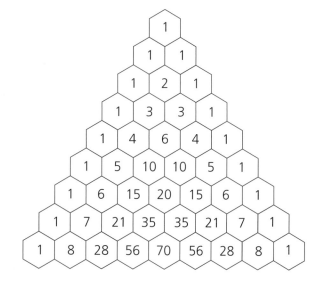

Sporting Goods

The chart shows the price of different pieces of sporting equipment. For each problem, circle the mathematical expression that matches the description.

S	Soccer balls	$22.00	P	Hockey pucks	$6.00
C	Cleats	$120.00	E	Helmets	$88.00
B	Baseball bats	$36.00	G	Golf clubs	$240.00
M	Baseball mitts	$59.00	I	Skis	$300.00
T	Basketballs	$18.00	K	Ski boots	$189.00
J	Jerseys	$45.00	O	Ski poles	$40.00
H	Hockey sticks	$39.00			

1. The cost of three helmets and two hockey sticks:

  a. $3(E + H)$

  b. $3E + 2H$

  c. $2E + 3H$

2. The cost of skis and four sets of ski poles:

  a. $I + 4O$

  b. $4I + O$

  c. $4(I + O)$

3. Ten dollars more than two basketballs:

  a. $2(T + 10)$

  b. $2(B + 10)$

  c. $2T + 10$

4. The cost of a pair of ski boots less $50.00:

  a. $50K$

  b. $50 + K$

  c. $K - 50$

5. The cost of golf clubs is greater than the cost of cleats:

  a. $G > C$

  b. $G < C$

  c. $G = C$

6. Three times the cost of both a baseball bat and a baseball mitt:

  a. $3B + M$

  b. $3 (B + M)$

  c. $3M + B$

7. Twenty dollars more than five hockey pucks:

  a. $5P + 20$

  b. $5(P + 20)$

  c. $20(5 + P)$

8. The cost of ski boots, skis, and two sets of ski poles is less than $600.

  a. $2K + I + O < 600$

  b. $K + I + 2O > 600$

  c. $K + I + 2O < 600$

Commutative Property

Write *true* or *false* to indicate if the following problems demonstrate the commutative property. If the example does *not* demonstrate the commutative property, explain why.

1. $4 + 5 = 5 + 4$

_____

2. $4 - 5 = 5 - 4$

_____

3. $5 \times 3 = 3 \times 5$

_____

4. $x + y = y + x$

_____

5. $x \div y = y \div x$

_____

6. $7 + 3 = 3 + 7$

_____

7. $4 \div 5 = 5 \div 4$

_____

8. $a \times b = b \times a$

_____

9. $(5 \times 4) \times 2 = 2 \times (5 \times 4)$

_____

10. $3 + (15 - 7) = (15 - 7) + 3$

_____

Figuring Out the World

Use the chart to solve the problems below.

Monthly World Population Figures	
07/01/07	6,600,411,051
08/01/07	6,606,949,106
09/01/07	6,613,487,162
10/01/07	6,619,814,313
11/01/07	6,626,352,369
12/01/07	6,632,679,520
01/01/08	6,639,217,576
02/01/08	6,645,755,632
03/01/08	6,651,871,878
04/01/08	6,658,409,934
05/01/08	6,664,737,085
06/01/08	6,671,275,141
07/01/08	6,677,602,292

1. Between which two months was there the smallest change in population? _____

_____

2. Round each of the population figures to the nearest hundred thousand.

_____   _____   _____

_____   _____   _____

_____   _____   _____

_____   _____   _____

_____

3. Write each of the first three population figures in the chart in expanded form.

_____

_____

_____

Fastball

Use the chart to solve the problems below.

Pitch	Pitch Speed (mph)	Result
1	98.2	swinging strike
2	99.1	swinging strike
3	98.7	ball
4	98.0	hit
5	97.9	foul
6	99.2	hit
7	99.6	swinging strike

1. What was the fastest pitch recorded? _____ What was its result? _____

2. What was the slowest pitch recorded? _____ What was its result? _____

3. Write the ratio of hits to swinging strikes. _____

4. Write the ratio of swinging strikes to the total number of results. _____

5. What is the mean of the pitch speeds recorded? _____

6. What is the median of the pitch speeds recorded? _____

Amazing Measurement

Help the mouse get to the cheese by finding the way through the maze. Use a ruler to make your lines straight. Then, use the correct path to solve the problems below.

1. Measure your path in inches. _____

2. How many centimeters is your path? _____

3. Based on your answers, how many centimeters are there in an inch? _____

4. If there are twelve inches in one foot, how many feet long is your path? Write your answer in feet and inches, for example 5 feet 6 inches or 5' 6". _____

Face Time

The shapes in the box are used to create the faces of three-dimensional figures. For each figure below, write the shape or shapes used to create each figure, and how many of each shape are required to do so. Don't forget to count the faces you cannot see!

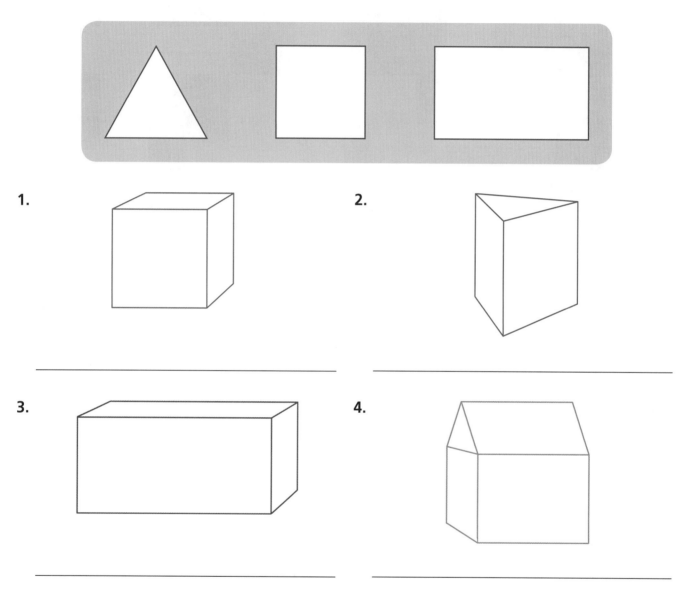

1.

_____

2.

_____

3.

_____

4.

_____

5.

_____

6.

_____

Moving the Pieces

Write out an equation that shows how to solve each problem.
Then rearrange it to demonstrate the commutative property, and write the answer.

1. Samantha had 53 marbles. Jason gave Samantha 15 additional marbles, then Samantha found another 3 marbles. How many marbles does Samantha have? _____

_____

_____

2. Max bought 6 bags of oranges from the grocery store. If each bag contains 8 oranges, how many oranges did he buy? _____

_____

3. There are 42 bookshelves in the bookstore. Each bookshelf has 6 rows of shelves. If 75 books can be stacked on each row of shelves, what is the total number of books in the bookstore?

_____

_____

4. In the morning, the puppy ate 3 treats given to it by its trainer. Then the treat bag fell over, and the puppy ate 6 more treats. Later in the day, its trainer gave the puppy 2 more treats. How many treats did the puppy eat that day? _____

_____

5. There are 3 compost bins at the Marshalls' house. Each one holds 1 quart of trash. How much trash can they collect altogether in their compost bins? _____

_____

Five-Day Forecast

Use the forecast to solve the problems below.

Monday	Tuesday	Wednesday	Thursday	Friday
High 81°F Low 65°F	**High 84°F** Low 64°F	**High 88°F** Low 69°F	**High 91°F** Low 72°F	**High 86°F** Low 65°F
Mostly cloudy. Scattered showers and thunderstorms in the morning. Then showers and thunderstorms likely in the afternoon. Highs in the low 80s. Southwest winds 5 to 10 mph. Chance of rain: 70 percent.	Showers and thunderstorms likely. Highs in the mid 80s. South winds 5 to 10 mph. Chance of rain: 60 percent.	Mostly cloudy and breezy. South winds 15 to 20 mph. Highs in the high 80s. Chance of rain: 10 percent.	Mostly sunny and clear. Highs in the low 90s.	Cloudy with scattered showers and thunderstorms. Lows in the mid 60s. Northwest winds around 5 mph. Chance of rain: 50 percent.

1. Which day has the highest predicted temperature? _____

2. Which day has the lowest predicted temperature? _____

3. Which day has the greatest difference between its high and low temperatures? _____

4. Which day would be the best to go to the beach and why? _____

_____

5. On which day is it most likely to rain? _____

6. What is the chance of rain on Wednesday? Express it as a fraction. _____

7. What is the chance of rain on Monday? Express it as a fraction. _____

8. What is the mean high temperature predicted? _____

9. What is the mean low temperature predicted? _____

10. Which day would be the best to fly a kite and why? _____

_____

If temperatures plummet in the late fall, what would the temperature be if . . .
(round your answers to the nearest tenth)

11. the high temperature was $\frac{1}{2}$ of Monday's high? _____

12. the low temperature was $\frac{3}{4}$ of Monday's low? _____

13. the high temperature was $\frac{2}{3}$ of Tuesday's high? _____

14. the low temperature was $\frac{4}{5}$ of Tuesday's low? _____

15. the high temperature was $\frac{2}{3}$ of Wednesday's high? _____

Make a Notation

Draw a line to connect each number to its match written in expanded notation.

4,205,891

30,432,840,110

5,234,765

4,523

295,002

4,000 + 500 + 20 + 3

200,000 + 90,000 + 5,000 + 2

30,000,000,000 + 400,000,000 + 30,000,000 + 2,000,000 + 800,000 + 40,000 + 100 + 10

5,000,000 + 200,000 + 30,000 + 4,000 + 700 + 60 + 5

4,000,000 + 200,000 + 5,000 + 800 + 90 + 1

Now, write the number represented by each of the following expanded notations.

1. 1,000,000 + 200,000 + 30,000 + 4,000 + 500 + 60 + 7

_____

2. 2,000,000 + 300,000 + 40,000 + 5,000 + 600 + 70 + 8

_____

3. 90,000,000 + 8,000,000 + 700,000 + 60,000 + 5,000 + 400 + 30 + 2

_____

4. 900,000 + 80,000 + 400 + 20 + 1

_____

5. 70,000,000 + 6,000,000 + 500,000 + 40,000 + 3,000 + 200 + 10

_____

Math Prefixes

Using the chart below, solve the problems that follow. Hint: use the prefix of each shape's name to help you.

Number of Sides	Shape
3	Triangle
4	Quadrilateral
5	Pentagon
6	Hexagon
7	Heptagon
8	Octagon
9	Nonagon
10	Decagon

1. How many legs does an octopus have? _____

2. The singing group was a trio. How many members did it have? _____

3. Mark competed in a decathlon. How many events did he compete in? _____

4. The pentarchy of countries each had its own ruler. How many countries were there? _____

5. The woman gave birth to quadruplets. How many babies did she have? _____

6. The hexapod insect crawled up the tree. How many feet did it have? _____

7. The litter of puppies was a heptad. How many puppies were in the litter? _____

8. Horses are quadrupeds. How many legs do they have? _____

9. How many horns did a triceratops have on its head? _____

10. The word was octosyllabic. How many syllables did it have? _____

Rainy Days

Follow the directions below to create your own line graph. Use the chart on page 69 to plot the points on your graph.

Label the x-axis MONTH.

Label the y-axis INCHES OF PRECIPITATION.

Label the x-axis with the 12 months of the year (January–December).

Label the y-axis with precipitation amounts from 0–7.00.

Month	Inches of Precipitation
Jan	2.57
Feb	2.40
Mar	3.74
Apr	2.98
May	4.06
June	5.58
July	5.19
Aug	3.88
Sept	4.34
Oct	3.88
Nov	3.30
Dec	2.72

Now use the information in the graph you created to answer the questions.

1. What was the total annual precipitation that year? _____

2. Which months were the wettest and driest? _____ _____

3. What was the mean amount of precipitation that year? _____

4. What was the mode for this graph? _____

5. What was the median for this graph? _____

Associative Property

Write *true* or *false* to indicate if the following problems demonstrate the associative property. If the example does *not* demonstrate the associative property, explain why.

1. $(x \times m) \times z = x \times (m \times z)$

_____

2. $(4 + 9) + 6 = 9 + (4 + 6)$

_____

3. $(x - y) - z = x - (y - z)$

_____

4. $3 \times (5 \times 10) = (3 \times 5) \times 10$

_____

5. $(2 \div 2) \div 4 = 2 \div (2 \div 4)$

_____

6. $(4 \times 5) \times 6 = 5 \times (4 \times 6)$

_____

7. $(x + y) + z = x + (y + z)$

_____

8. $(x \div y) \div z = x \div (y \div z)$

_____

9. $4 \times (8 \times 6) = (4 \times 8) \times 6$

_____

10. $(4 - 5) - 6 = 4 - (5 - 6)$

_____

The Cookie Jar

Answer the following questions. Write your answers as whole numbers or fractions.

1. The cookie jar contains 12 cookies. If each person has $\frac{3}{4}$ of a cookie, how many people can eat the cookies? _____

2. Some of the cookies have been eaten. If $\frac{3}{4}$ of 12 cookies are left, how many are there? _____

3. If 12 cookies are split in $\frac{1}{2}$, how many people can have cookies? _____

4. If there are 16 cookies in the cookie jar and each person eats $\frac{1}{4}$ of a cookie, how many people can have some? _____

5. If you want to double a cookie recipe that calls for $\frac{1}{4}$ cup of butter, how much butter should you use? _____

6. The cookie jar falls on the ground! Of the 20 cookies inside, $\frac{1}{6}$ are eaten by the dog. How many are left? _____

7. There are 24 cookies in the jar, and each person eats $1\frac{1}{3}$ cookies. How many people can have some? _____

8. If you take $4\frac{3}{4}$ cookies, but eat only $2\frac{1}{2}$ of them, how much is left? _____

Check the Frequency

Pick one sentence out of a newspaper and chart how many times each letter appears within the sentence. Use the chart below.

Letter	Number of Times It Appears	Letter	Number of Times It Appears
A		N	
B		O	
C		P	
D		Q	
E		R	
F		S	
G		T	
H		U	
I		V	
J		W	
K		X	
L		Y	
M		Z	

Which letter occurred most often? _____

Which vowel occurred most often? _____

Which consonant occurred most often? _____

Pick a second sentence out of a newspaper and chart how many times each letter appears within the sentence. Use the chart below.

Letter	Number of Times It Appears	Letter	Number of Times It Appears
A		N	
B		O	
C		P	
D		Q	
E		R	
F		S	
G		T	
H		U	
I		V	
J		W	
K		X	
L		Y	
M		Z	

Which letter occurred most often? _____

Which vowel occurred most often? _____

Which consonant occurred most often? _____

How does this compare to the first frequency chart? _____

_____

Pick a third sentence out of a newspaper and chart how many times each letter
appears within the sentence. Use the chart below.

Letter	Number of Times It Appears	Letter	Number of Times It Appears
A		N	
B		O	
C		P	
D		Q	
E		R	
F		S	
G		T	
H		U	
I		V	
J		W	
K		X	
L		Y	
M		Z	

Which letter occurred most often? _____

Which vowel occurred most often? _____

Which consonant occurred most often? _____

How does this compare to the first and second frequency charts? _____

_____

_____

Shaping Up

Draw a line to match each shape to its description.

one angle = 90°

2 equal sides, 2 equal angles

both pairs of opposite sides equal and parallel, no right angles

opposite sides equal, 4 right angles

one pair of opposite sides parallel

symmetric about any diameter

4 equal sides, 4 right angles

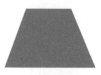

3 equal sides, 3 equal angles

4 equal sides, opposite sides parallel, no right angles

Circular Reasoning

Use the figure below to answer the questions that follow.

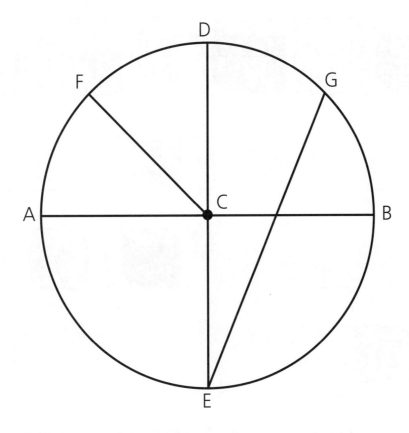

1. What is the center point of the circle called? _____

2. Name two diameters on this circle. _____ _____

3. Line CF is called what? _____

4. Name one acute central angle in the circle. _____

5. Line EG is called what? _____

6. What is AE called? _____

7. If line DC measures 4 inches, what does line FC measure? _____

8. If line AC measures 4 inches, what does line AB measure? _____

9. What is the measurement of angle DCB? _____

10. Use a protractor to measure angle DEG. Write its measurement here. _____

Chancing It

Blocks are picked at random from the group below. Figure out the probability of picking the blocks that follow.

1.  _____

2. B _____

3. C _____

4. A or B _____

5. B or C _____

Now use the spinners to answer the following probability questions.

A   **B**   **C**

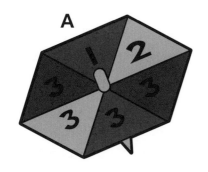 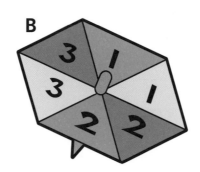 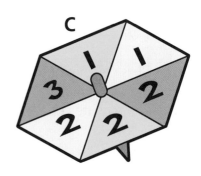

6. Which spinner shows a probability of spinning a 2 as $\frac{1}{3}$? _____

7. Which spinner shows a probability of spinning a 3 as $\frac{1}{6}$? _____

8. Which spinner shows a probability of spinning a 1 as $\frac{1}{6}$? _____

9. If you win the game by spinning a 3, which spinner should you choose? _____

10. If you win the game by spinning a 2, which spinner should you choose? _____

Algebra Lingo

It's much easier to understand algebra if you understand the terms used in it.
Use the example below to help you solve the problems.

$$7z + 18m$$

term   coefficient   variable

How many *variables* are there in each of these expressions?

1. $3a + 5a$ _____

2. $2z - 6x$ _____

3. $p + v - 2x$ _____

What are the *terms* in each of these expressions?

4. $3a + 2t$ _____

5. $2n + n + 7k$ _____

6. $3p$ _____

Are the terms in these expressions *like* or *unlike*? Indicate this with an *L* or a *U*.

7. $6x + 2x$ _____

8. $-3a - 5v$ _____

9. $9s + 2(x + t)$ _____

What are the *coefficients* in these expressions?

10. $9z$ _____

11. $\frac{1}{2}r$ _____

12. $7c$ _____

Decimal Sleuth

Circle the number in each group that meets all the criteria outlined.

1. The number is larger than 26.5.

The number in the tens place is three larger than the number in the tenths place.

The digit in the ones place is not 2.

56.2
72.4
24.9
35.2

2. Every digit in the number is odd.

Each digit is different from the others.

The digit in the hundredths place is 3.

1.51
5.73
7.51
3.23

3. Every digit is even.

Each digit is different from the others.

The sum of the digits is 16.

4.26
6.86
2.86 1.84
5.83

4. When rounded to the nearest whole number, the number is 24.

The digit in the hundredths place is 7.

The digit in the tenths place is 8.

23.87
24.87
24.37
24.03

5. The digit in the hundredths place is 2.

All of the digits are even.

Rounded to the nearest whole number, the number is not 5.

4.823
8.224
6.482
4.824

6. The number in the tenths place is 6.

Rounded to the nearest whole number, the number is 46.

The sum of the digits is 24.

45.67
46.02
43.65
45.69

7. The number contains a 0.

The number in the tenths place has a value.

The number contains a 2.

0.2
0.3
1.0
1.2

8. The number contains three 5s.

The number in the thousandths place is 5.

The sum of the first three digits is 6.

345.555
234.555
123.555
985.550

Evaluating Measurements

Compare each set of measurements by using the **<**, **>**, or **=** symbols. If the expression is not equal, make it equal by changing one of the measurements.

1. 3 quarts _____ 9 gallons

_____

2. 16 ounces _____ 1 pound

_____

3. 6 yards _____ 18 feet

_____

4. 3 pounds _____ 33 ounces

_____

5. 2,000 pounds _____ 1 ton

_____

6. 2 cups _____ 1 pint

_____

7. 2 yards _____ 60 inches

_____

8. 5 gallons _____ 18 quarts

_____

9. 4 feet _____ 48 inches

_____

10. 5 pints _____ 2 quarts

_____

Admittance Fee

There are several theme parks within driving distance of the Welder family. Help the family evaluate their options by answering the questions below. For each question, list the operation(s) required to solve the problem, then provide an answer.

	Seven Flags	Dreamworld	Galaxy Studios
Adult Daily Entrance Fee	$39.99	$71.00	$59.00
Child Daily Entrance Fee	$29.99	$60.00	$39.00
Adult Season Pass	$79.00	$215.00	$180.00
Child Season Pass	$59.00	$185.00	$120.00

1. What is the cost of four adult daily passes to Dreamworld? _____

2. What is the cost of two adult daily tickets and one child daily ticket to Galaxy Studios?

_____

3. Four adult friends want to go to Seven Flags for one day. Can they do this for less than $200.00?

_____

4. How many times does an adult have to go to Dreamworld to make a season pass worth the cost? _____

5. You want to go to one of the parks for three days. There will be two adults and two children. Which park is the best value? _____

6. How many times does a child have to go to Galaxy Studios to make a season pass worth the cost? _____

7. How much will you save if one adult and one child go to Galaxy Studios for a day compared to going to Dreamworld? _____

8. You want to buy four season passes to Dreamworld: one adult and three child passes. Can you do this for less than $800.00? _____

Lost

Use the map below to help the lost campers find their way.

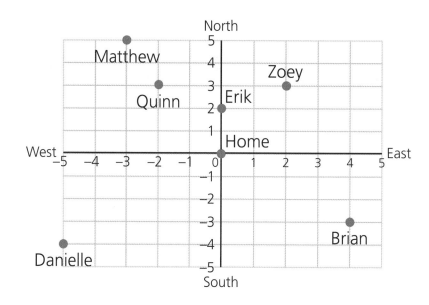

1. Which ordered pair best represents Zoey's location?

  a. (1,3)

  b. (2,3)

  c. (3,2)

  d. (1,−3)

2. Which ordered pair best represents Brian's location?

  a. (4,−3)

  b. (−3,4)

  c. (−3,3)

  d. (−4,−2)

3. Which ordered pair best represents Quinn's location?

  a. (−2,2)

  b. (2,−3)

  c. (−2,3)

  d. (3,1)

4. Which ordered pair best represents Matthew's location?

  a. (5,−3)

  b. (−3,5)

  c. (3,5)

  d. (−3,−5)

5. Which camper is closest to home?

_____

6. If Danielle walked five units east and 4 units north, where would she be? _____

7. If Brian walked one unit south and nine units west, where would he be? _____

8. Another camper, named Charlotte, is lost, too! She is two units south and two units west of Erik. Mark her location on the map and label it.

Body Estimates

The page on which you are writing is $8\frac{1}{2}$ inches wide. Using this as a guide, fill in the chart below by estimating the length of things and then checking it with a ruler or tape measure.

What to Measure	Estimate	Actual Measurement
Width of your palm		
Length of your leg from hip to ankle		
Arm span from fingertip to fingertip		
Length of your arm from elbow to wrist		
Length of your index finger		
Width of your shoulders		

How did your estimates compare to the actual measurements? _____

_____

_____

_____

3-D Shape-Up

Draw a line to match each three-dimensional shape to its description.

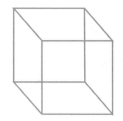

all slanted edges are equal length, square base

all four faces are triangles

all side lengths equal, square faces, all right angles

all points on surface equidistant from center

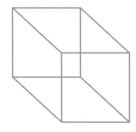

cross section remains the same throughout shape

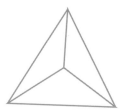

circular base

Road Signs

Use the road signs to determine if the equations are correct or incorrect. Write *correct* or *incorrect* for each problem. If the equation is incorrect, rewrite it to make it correct.

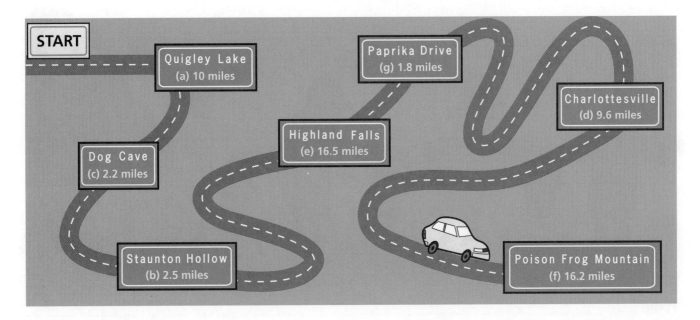

1. $\frac{f}{10} = 1.46$ _____

2. $0.2c - b = 6.4$ _____

3. $a + g = c + d$ _____

4. $\frac{a}{4} = b$ _____

5. $d + e - c = f - 7.7$ _____

6. $2(d - 1.5) = f$ _____

7. $e = 3(b + 3)$ _____

8. You drive to Quigley Lake but backtrack 3.6 miles. How many miles are you from where you started? _____

9. You drive one-third of the way up Poison Frog Mountain from Charlottesville. How many miles have you traveled? _____

10. You drive to Charlottesville and back again twice. How many miles have you traveled?

_____

Distributive Property

Change the following expressions to represent the distributive property. Then provide an answer, if possible.

1. $4(a + b)$ _____

2. $7(2c - 3d + 5)$ _____

3. $7 \times (5 + 3)$ _____

4. $2a + 2b$ _____

5. $(a - 3)(b + 4)$ _____

6. $5 \times (2 + 3)$ _____

7. $(x - 5)(z + 2)$ _____

8. $7(2a + 3b)$ _____

9. $3(2c - 2d + 4)$ _____

10. $10c - 20d + 30$ _____

Cookie Culprit

Who took the last cookie from the cookie jar? Read the story and solve the problems.

Martin came home from school at 2 PM today. Mrs. Lindgren returned home with Jackie 2 hours after Martin came home. Martin's friend James came over to play 1 hour after Martin came home from school. Dad came home from work while Mrs. Lindgren was cooking supper 2 hours after she brought Jackie home. Martin, James, Jackie, Mrs. Lindgren, Mr. Lindgren, and Grandma Lindgren ate dinner at 7:30 PM. Dinner lasted 45 minutes. After dinner, Mr. and Mrs. Lindgren, Jackie, Martin, and James went into the living room together. At 9 PM, Mrs. Lindgren went upstairs and knocked on a bedroom door. A voice from inside told her to enter. There, Grandma Lindgren, who was home all day, sat in her rocker with a glass of milk in her hand and crumbs in her lap.

1. Who came home at 2 PM? _____

2. Who came home at 4 PM? _____

3. What time did Mr. Lindgren come home? _____

4. What time did James come over? _____

5. Who was at home at 3 PM? _____

6. Who was at home at 2:15 PM? _____

7. How much time passed between the time James came over and the time Mr. Lindgren came home? _____

8. Who is the cookie culprit? _____

Identity and Zero Properties

Any number multiplied by 1 remains the same. This is the multiplicative identity. Any number plus zero remains the same. This is called the additive identity. Identify which property was used in each equation. Complete the equations below.

1. _____ + 4 = 4

2. 0 + _____ = 2

3. 5 × _____ = 5

4. 1 × _____ = 3

5. _____ + 8 = 8

6. 11 × 1 = _____

7. _____ + 0 = 12

8. 12 = 1 × _____

9. 6 + _____ = 6

10. 6 = 6 × _____

Table Tricks

Choose the equation that was used to make the function table.

1.

x	y
–9	–5
–2	2
4	8
11	15

a. $y = \dfrac{x}{2}$

b. $y = 2x$

c. $y = x - 4$

d. $y = x + 4$

2.

x	y
–5	0
–1	4
0	5
5	10

a. $y = 5 + x$

b. $y = \dfrac{x}{5}$

c. $y = 5x$

d. $y = 5 - x$

3.

x	y
–2	–6
–1	–3
0	0
1	3

a. $y = x + 3$

b. $y = 3x$

c. $y = x - 3$

d. $y = \dfrac{x}{3}$

4.

x	y
–6	–2
–3	–1
3	1
12	4

a. $y = x + 3$

b. $y = 3x$

c. $y = \dfrac{x}{3}$

d. $y = x - 3$

5.

x	y
–3	–6
–2	–4
1	2
4	8

a. $y = 2 + x$

b. $y = 2 - x$

c. $y = 2x$

d. $y = \dfrac{x}{2}$

6.

x	y
–8	–2
0	6
4	10
7	13

a. $y = 6x$

b. $y = 6 + x$

c. $y = \dfrac{x}{6}$

d. $y = x - 6$

Create a function table for each equation.

7. $y = x - 6$

8. $y = \dfrac{x}{8}$

Moving Images

Use the images to solve the problems below.

1. Which image does *not* show a reflection?

a. 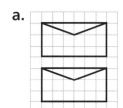 b. 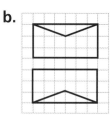 c. 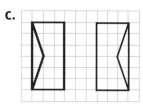 d.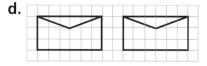

2. Which of these images shows a reflection?

a.  b. 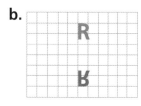 c. 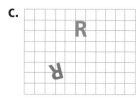 d.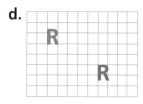

3. Which of these images shows a rotation?

a.  b.  c.  d.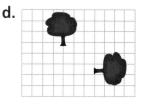

4. Which of these images does *not* show a rotation?

a. 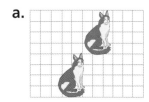 b. 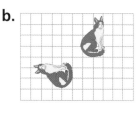 c. 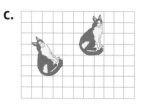 d.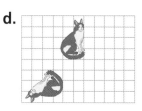

5. Which of these images shows a translation?

a.  b.  c.  d.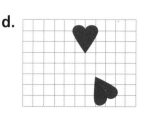

Finding Patterns

Look for the pattern in the sequences below.

1. 25, 32, 28, 35, 31, 38

Which rule describes this pattern best? _____

2. 11, 7, 10, 6, 9, 5

Which rule describes this pattern best? _____

3. 5, 10, 15, 20, 25, 30

Which rule describes this pattern best? _____

4. 17, 14, 24, 21, 31, 28

Which rule describes this pattern best? _____

5. –5, –2, –3, 0, –1, 2

Which rule describes this pattern best? _____

6. Create a number pattern in which you add 7.

_____

7. Create a number pattern in which you add 10, subtract 4.

_____

8. Create a number pattern in which you add 1, subtract 6.

_____

9. Create a number pattern in which you subtract 9, add 5.

_____

10. Create a number pattern in which you subtract 12, add 15.

_____

Snack Shack

Everybody's eating at the Snack Shack. Use the menu to solve the problems below.
Round your answers to the nearest penny.

JACK'S SNACK SHACK

Taco $1.25
Hot Dog $2.50
Hamburger $3.25
Cheeseburger $3.50
Chili small $2.00
      large $3.50
Fries $2.25

Onion Rings $2.00
Side Salad $3.75
Pizza Slice $1.75
Bottled Water $1.50
Soda $1.75
Iced Tea $1.95

1. Table 1 orders 1 cheeseburger, 1 basket of fries, 1 diet soda, 1 large chili, 2 bottles of water, and a side salad. What is the total cost before tax and tip? _____

2. Table 2 orders 2 iced teas, 2 slices of pizza, and 2 side salads. What is the total cost before tax and tip?_____ If tax is 5%, how much tax does Table 2 owe? _____

3. Table 3 orders 1 small chili, 3 slices of pizza, 2 side salads, and 4 sodas. What is the total cost before tax and tip?_____ If tax is 8%, how much tax does Table 3 owe? _____

4. Table 4 orders 6 cheeseburgers, 4 baskets of fries, 5 onion rings, 2 bottles of water, and 3 iced teas. What is the total cost before tax and tip?_____ If Table 4 has a coupon for 5% off their bill before tax and tip, what is their new total bill after the coupon has been applied? _____

5. Table 5 orders 5 tacos, 2 sodas, 1 basket of fries, and 1 small chili. What is the total bill before tax and tip? _____ If Table 5 has a coupon for 10% off their bill before tax and tip, what is their new total bill after the coupon has been applied? _____

6. Table 6 orders 4 hamburgers, 1 cheeseburger, 5 baskets of fries, and 5 sodas. What is the total bill before tax and tip? _____ If Table 6 has a coupon for 15% off their bill before tax and tip, what is their new total bill after the coupon has been applied? _____ If tax is 5% of the new total, how much tax does Table 6 owe? _____

7. Table 7 orders 2 tacos, 2 side salads, 1 hamburger, 2 baskets of fries, 3 hot dogs, 1 small chili, 2 sodas, 1 bottled water, and 1 iced tea. What is the total bill? _____ If Table 7 has a coupon for 10% off their bill before tax and tip, what is their new total bill after the coupon has been applied? _____ If tax is 7% of the new total bill, how much tax does Table 7 owe? _____ If Table 7 wants to leave a tip of 20% before tax, how much tip should they leave? _____

8. Table 8 is an entire sports team! They order 25 hamburgers, 5 cheeseburgers, 15 baskets of fries, 10 onion rings, 5 side salads, 30 bottles of water, and 30 small chilis. What is their total bill? _____ If Table 8 has a coupon for 20% off their bill, what is their new total bill after the coupon has been applied? _____ If tax is 5.5% of the new total bill, how much tax does Table 8 owe? _____ If Table 8 wants to leave a tip of 15% before tax, how much tip should they leave? _____ How much money has Table 8 paid out in total? _____

Things in Common

Write five common multiples for each set of numbers below.

1. 3, 15 _____

2. 3, 7 _____

3. 5, 6 _____

4. 16, 2 _____

5. 4, 5 _____

Find the *least* common multiple for the following numbers.

6. 12, 20 _____

7. 10,15 _____

8. 3, 5, 12 _____

9. 4, 7, 9 _____

10. 150, 375 _____

11. In a basketball game, the Titans scored all 2-pointers, while the opposing team, the Bulldogs, scored all 3-pointers. Can the score be tied 18 to 18? _____

12. Time for Tennis ships their tennis balls in units of 6, while Tennis Pro Shop ships their tennis balls in units of 8. What is the fewest number of tennis balls you would need to order to receive the same number of tennis balls from each company in full units? _____

13. Weightlifter Will has 5-pound weights on his bar. Weightlifter Wendy has 12-pound weights on her bar. What is the lowest amount of weight each weightlifter would need on his or her bar to be lifting the same amount? _____

14. The Giants scored an extra point for each touchdown they made in the football game, for a total of seven points each time they scored. The Eagles did not score an extra point for any of their touchdowns, so they got 6 points every time they scored. The game ended in a tie. What was the score? _____

15. In the situation in the previous problem, assume that the Giants also scored a field goal worth three points. What would be the lowest score at which the teams could still tie? _____

Match the Photo

Draw a line to match each person's name to the picture frame containing his or her photo.
Fill in any missing information. *P* stands for perimeter and *A* stands for area.

MAX

P = _____ cm, *A* = 25 cm

SUSAN

P = 14 cm, *A* = _____ cm

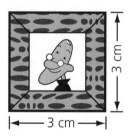

HARRY

P = 12 cm, *A* = _____ cm

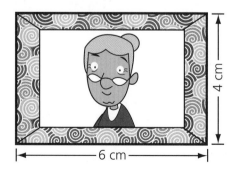

ROSE

P = _____ cm, *A* = 24 cm

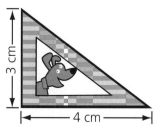

HIGGINS

P = 12 cm, *A* = _____ cm

Budget Buster

The chart shows how Marla spends her $800 monthly earnings. Use the chart to answer the following questions. Round monetary answers to the nearest cent.

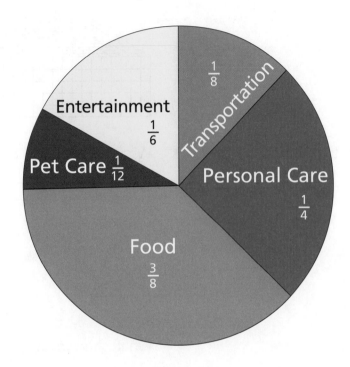

1. On what does Marla spend the largest amount of money? _____
On what does Marla spend the least amount of money? _____

2. How much money does Marla spend on personal care each month? _____

3. How much money does Marla spend on food each month? _____

4. How much money does Marla spend on pet care each month? _____

5. How much money does Marla spend on transportation and entertainment each month, combined? _____

6. Marla has one dog. If she got a second dog, what area of her monthly budget would increase and by about how much? _____

7. If Marla reduced what she spends on personal care to $100 per month, what fraction of her earnings could she save? _____

8. If Marla ate at home once more each month, she would save $30. What fraction of her current food expenditure would she be saving? _____

Voluminous

Answer the volume questions that follow. Round your answers to the nearest hundredths.

1.

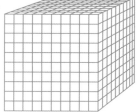

What is the volume of this prism?

_____

2.

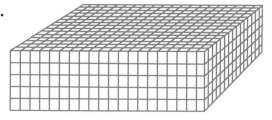

What is the volume of this prism?

_____

3.

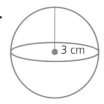

What is the volume of this sphere?

_____

4.

What is the volume of this cone?

_____

5.

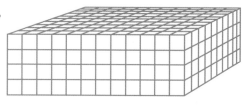

What is the volume of this prism?

_____

6.

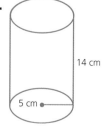

What is the volume of this cylinder?

_____

7.

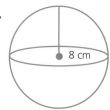

What is the volume of this sphere?

_____

8.

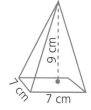

What is the volume of this pyramid?

_____

Extracurricular Activities

Use the diagrams below to solve the problems.

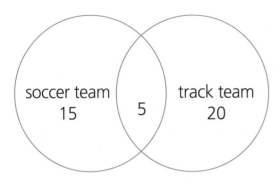

1. How many students are only on the soccer team?

_____

2. How many students are only on the track team?

_____

3. How many students are on both the soccer and track teams? _____

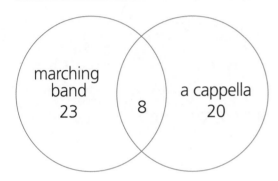

4. How many students are only in the marching band?

_____

5. How many students are in both the marching band and the a cappella group? _____

6. How many students are in the a cappella group but not in the marching band? _____

Draw a Venn diagram to represent each of the following situations.

7. There are 12 students that participate only in the volunteer club, 9 students that participate only in the future leaders club, and 4 students that participate in both clubs.

8. There are 9 students that participate in the math team, 6 students that participate in the drama club, and 3 students that participate in both.

Dressing the Part

Use the images to solve the problems below.

1. A fraction of the group of students below is wearing a dark shirt.

Which of the following is shaded to represent a fraction with the same value?

a.    **b.**    **c.**

2. A fraction of the group of students below is wearing a scarf.

Which of the following is shaded to represent a fraction with the same value?

a.    **b.**    **c.**

3. A fraction of the group of students below is wearing shorts.

Which of the following is shaded to represent a fraction with the same value?

a.    **b.**    **c.**

4. A fraction of the group of students below is wearing brown shoes.

Which of the following is shaded to represent a fraction with the same value?

a.   **b.**   **c.**

Best in Show

Use the graph to solve the problems below.

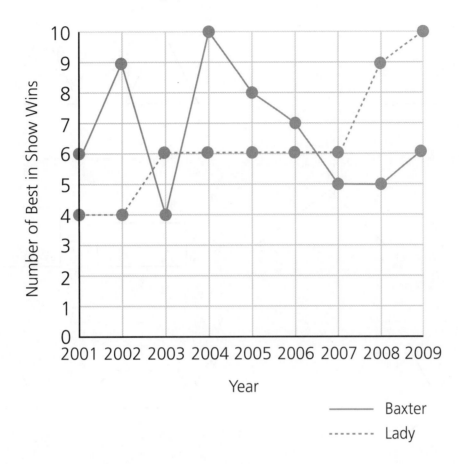

Year

——— Baxter

------ Lady

1. Through 2004, which dog had the most Best in Show wins? _____

2. How many more Best in Show wins did Lady have in her best year compared to her worst?

_____

3. Which dog had the greatest increase in Best in Show wins between 2001 and 2002? _____

4. Which dog had the largest increase in Best in Show wins in any one-year period? _____

5. Did the dogs ever have the same number of Best in Show wins in the same year? _____

6. Who had the most Best in Show wins in 2009? _____

7. Who had the most Best in Show wins in the entire time period shown? _____

8. For what year is the following equation true? Baxter − Lady = 5 _____

Similar Congruence

For each set of shapes, write whether they are *congruent*, *similar*, or *neither*.

1.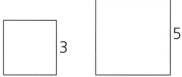

_____

2.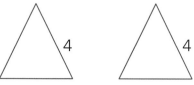

_____

3.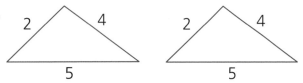

_____

4.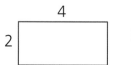

_____

5.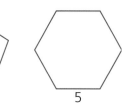

_____

6.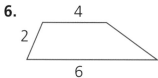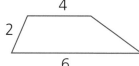

_____

7.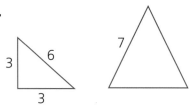

_____

8.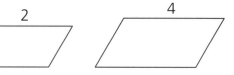

_____

9.

_____

10.

_____

Skyline Peak

Use the chart of average monthly temperatures at Skyline Peak to solve the problems below.

Month	Daytime Temperature	Nighttime Temperature
January	22°F	11°F
February	28°F	15°F
March	38°F	18°F
April	44°F	26°F
May	56°F	34°F
June	67°F	42°F
July	74°F	49°F
August	70°F	40°F
September	62°F	37°F
October	49°F	27°F
November	39°F	20°F
December	26°F	17°F

1. Nighttime Temp = July's Daytime Temp − 40 _____

2. Nighttime Temp = $\frac{1}{2}$ its Daytime Temp _____

3. Daytime Temp = 30 + its own Nighttime Temp _____

4. Daytime to Nighttime Temp ratio is equivalent to 7:4. _____

5. Daytime to Nighttime Temp ratio is equivalent to 19:9. _____

6. What is the mean Daytime Temperature for the year to the nearest whole degree? _____

7. What is the median Nighttime Temperature for the year? _____

8. What is the mode for the entire chart? _____

Money Matters

Answer the money questions below.

1. Penelope bought a piece of candy and received $0.42 in change. What is the smallest number of coins she could have received as change? _____

2. Clinton purchased a cup of coffee and received $0.72 in change. What is the smallest number of coins he could have received as change? _____

3. José bought lunch for $4.89 and paid with a five-dollar bill. What is the smallest number of coins he could have received as change? _____

4. Maxine purchased dinner for $15.65 and paid with a 20-dollar bill. What is the smallest number of paper bills she could have received as change? _____

5. Stacy bought a sweater for $40.99. What is the smallest number of paper bills she could have used to pay? _____

6. Alban bought a soda that cost $2.11 and paid with a 20-dollar bill. What is the smallest combination of paper bills and coins he could have received as change? _____

7. Dara received $0.52 as change. What combination of coins is the fewest she could have received as change? _____
What combination of coins is the most she could have received as change? _____
_____

8.

What amount of money is represented here? _____
What is the smallest combination of coins you could use to make the same amount of money?
_____

Temperature Change

To convert Fahrenheit temperatures to the Celsius scale, we use this formula:

$$°C = (°F - 32)\frac{5}{9}$$

The formula is completed in two simple steps.

Step 1: Subtract 32°

Step 2: Multiply the result by $\frac{5}{9}$ (or 0.56)

> For example: 98.6°F
>
> 1. $98.6 - 32 = 66.6$
> 2. $66.6 \times \frac{5}{9} = \frac{333}{9} = 37°C$

Now change the following Fahrenheit temperatures to Celsius. Round your answers to the nearest whole degree.

1. 66°F _____

2. 25°F _____

3. 94°F _____

4. 55°F _____

5. 12°F _____

6. Using what you know about Fahrenheit to Celsius conversion, how do you think Celsius temperatures can be converted to Fahrenheit ones? Write a formula for how to do this.

_____

Convert these Celsius temperatures to Fahrenheit.

7. 27°C _____

8. −16°C _____

9. 40°C _____

10. −4°C _____

Deductive Reasoning

Use deductive reasoning to solve the problems.

1. A movie is being shown at the following times: 11 AM, 1 PM, 3 PM, 5 PM, and 7 PM. Antonio went to see a movie before 5 PM. He did not see a morning show. Antonio ate lunch at 2:45, after the movie had let out. What showing did Antonio attend? _____

2. Mike's birthday is the day after tomorrow. Yesterday was Wednesday. What day is Mike's birthday? _____

3. Three friends ran a marathon together. Carmen finished before Amber. Martin finished first. Who finished last? _____

4. Betsy is taller than Elsa. Elsa is taller than Lucia. Who is taller, Betsy or Lucia? _____

5. There are four children in a family. Their ages are 5, 7, 17, and 19. Erik is the oldest. Danielle is not younger than Mark. Matthew is the youngest. How old is Danielle? _____

6. Maribel planted a garden with a row of carrots, a row of squash, and a row of tomatoes. The tomatoes were to the right of the squash. The carrots were to the left of the squash. What was planted left of the tomatoes? _____

All Shapes and Sizes

Draw a line to match each description to its shape.

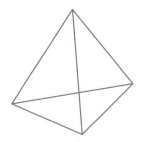

This figure has 4 faces, 4 vertices, and 6 edges.

This figure has 3 more edges than vertices or faces.

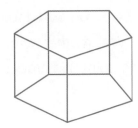

This figure has 5 faces, 6 vertices, and 9 edges.

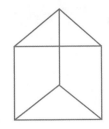

This figure has a circular base.

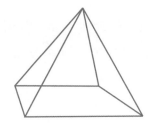

This figure has 15 edges.

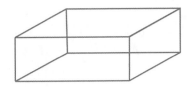

This figure has 2 more vertices than faces.

The Right Angles

Use a straight edge and a protractor to finish drawing each angle.

1. Points X and Y have been connected to make one side of an angle. Which other point should you connect to point X in order to make a 45° angle?

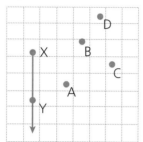

2. Points A and B have been connected to make one side of an angle. Which other point should you connect to point A in order to make a 25° angle?

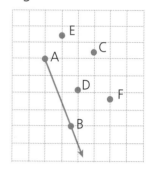

3. Points X and Y have been connected to make one side of an angle. Which other point should you connect to point X in order to make a 95° angle?

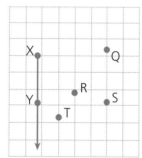

4. Points B and C have been connected to make one side of an angle. Which other point should you connect to point B in order to make a 130° angle?

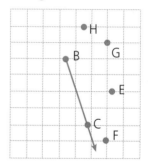

5. Points X and Y have been connected to make one side of an angle. Which other point should you connect to point X in order to make a 168° angle?

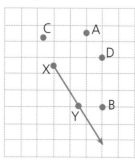

6. Points J and K have been connected to make one side of an angle. Which other point should you connect to point J in order to make a 60° angle?

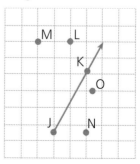

Your Day

Tomorrow, keep track of every hour of your day. Use the chart below to log what activities fill up your day and how many hours you spend doing them. Don't forget to include sleeping!

Activity	Amount of Time

Now, using your log of daily activities, fill in the pie chart below to illustrate what portion of your day you spend doing different things. Each portion represents one hour of a day. Label the chart with the activity and what fraction it represents.

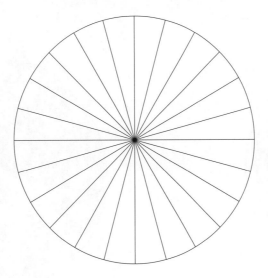

What activity takes up the most time in your day? _____

What takes up the least amount of time? _____

Was there an activity that takes up more time than you realized? _____

Thinking in Circles

Solve the problems about circles. Round your answers to the nearest hundredth.

1.

r = 12 inches

If the radius of a softball is 12 inches, what is its circumference? _____

2.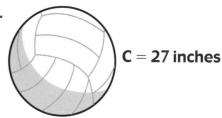

C = 27 inches

The circumference of a volleyball is 27 inches. What is its diameter? _____

3.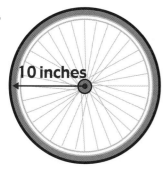

10 inches

If the radius of a bicycle tire is 10 inches, what is its circumference? _____

4. D = 1.7 inches

A golf ball has a diameter of 1.7 inches. What is the circumference? _____

5.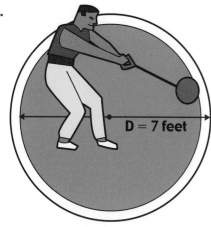

D = 7 feet

In the track and field hammer throw event, the hammer throw circle has a diameter of 7 feet. What is the circumference? _____

6.

C = 20 meters

If an equestrian circle has a circumference of 20 meters, what is its diameter? _____

Simple Interest

When money is borrowed, interest is charged for the use of that money. When the money is paid back, the principal, or amount of money that was borrowed, is paid back, plus interest. The amount of interest depends on the interest rate, the amount of money borrowed, and the length of time that the money is borrowed. Use the formulas in the box to solve the problems below.

> The formula for finding simple interest is:
>
> Interest = Principal × Rate × Time
>
> The amount of interest owed is added to the amount of money borrowed to determine the total amount paid to the lender.
>
> Principal + Interest = Total Owed to Lender

1. Marcus borrowed $500.00 over 2 years at a rate of 5%. What is the principal in this scenario? _____ What is the interest rate in this scenario? _____ What is the time in this scenario? _____

2. Rupal borrowed $3,500.00 over 5 years at a rate of 15%. How much interest will she owe?

_____

3. Jessica borrowed $12,000.00 over 8 years at a rate of 7.5%. How much interest will she owe?

_____

4. If Shane owes $1,500.00 in interest, and she borrowed $10,000.00 over 3 years, what was the interest rate? _____

5. If Rita owes $3,150.00 in interest, and she paid it over 6 years at a rate of 7%, what was the principal? _____

6. If Ming owes $510,000.00 in interest and borrowed $200,000.00 at 8.5%, how long was her loan? _____

7. If Elias borrowed $4,000.00 over 5 years at a rate of 10%, how much interest does he owe and how much does he owe the lender in total? _____

8. If Isobel borrowed $800.00 over 1 year at a rate of 11%, how much interest does she owe and how much does she owe the lender in total? _____

Clocking In

Using the information in the time sheet, fill in the blank spaces. Then solve the problems on the next page.

Employee	Time In	Time Out	Number of Hours Worked	Hourly Wage	Total Wage Earned
Nina	7:00 AM		10	$7.50	$75.00
Jerry	6:50 AM	4:20 PM		$6.95	$66.03
Neo	7:07 AM	4:07 PM	9	$8.00	
Cheyenne	7:45 AM	5:45 PM	10		$75.00
Scott		4:30 PM	8	$8.25	$66.00
Elan	8:01 AM		$10\frac{1}{2}$	$9.50	$99.75
Waldorf		4:35 PM	9	$9.00	$81.00
Dashon	8:10 AM	4:40 PM		$7.75	$65.88
Oscar	7:55 AM	4:55 PM	9		$72.00
Harper	7:20 AM	3:50 PM	$8\frac{1}{2}$	$6.95	
Lee	7:57 AM	5:57 PM		$9.25	$92.50

1. Who is the highest paid employee? _____

2. Which employee worked the fewest hours that day? _____

3. Which employee stayed the latest that evening? _____

4. Which employee arrived the earliest that morning? _____

5. Which employee earned the least money that day? _____

6. What is the mode wage? _____

7. What is the mean wage? Round to the nearest cent. _____

8. If Harper had stayed 30 minutes longer that day, how much would she have earned? _____

9. If Waldorf earned $0.50 more per hour, how much would he have earned? _____

10. If Oscar took 30 minutes off of unpaid time that day, how much money would he have lost?

_____

Weighty Measures

Use your knowledge of weight measurement to solve the problems.

1. Which unit would most often be used to determine the mass of a piece of notebook paper?

    a. kilogram

    b. gram

    c. meter

    d. liter

2. Which unit would most often be used to determine the weight of a cell phone?

    a. ounce

    b. pound

    c. gram

    d. liter

3. Which unit would most often be used to determine the weight of an elephant?

    a. meter

    b. ounce

    c. gram

    d. ton

4. Which unit would most often be used to determine the volume of a pitcher of water?

    a. meter

    b. liter

    c. gram

    d. pound

5. Which unit would most often be used to determine the length of a track?

    a. gram

    b. kilogram

    c. ounce

    d. meter

6. Which unit would most often be used to determine the weight of a dog?

    a. pound

    b. meter

    c. liter

    d. gram

Circle the weight of the object pictured.

7.

    4 ounces

    4 pounds

8.

    1.62 ounces

    1.62 pounds

9.

    3,000 pounds

    3,000 tons

10.

    5 ounces

    5 pounds

Probability Problems

Based on the situation described, circle each question that could be answered using probability.

1. In a classroom, there are 5 students with red hair, 8 students with blond hair, and 9 students with brown hair.

   a. How many students are in the class all together?

   b. If the teacher picks 1 student at random, what color hair is that student most likely to have?

   c. How many more students have brown hair than red hair?

   d. If the teacher buys 2 pencils for each student, how many pencils will she buy?

2. At Kennedy Middle School, 3 out of 5 students make honor roll.

   a. If the principal awards each honor roll student a plaque, how many plaques are needed?

   b. What is the likelihood that a student will not make honor roll?

   c. What percentage of students will make honor roll?

   d. How many students attend Kennedy Middle School?

3. In a class of 30 students, there are 17 girls and 13 boys. There are 5 A students, and 3 of these students are girls.

   a. If a student is chosen at random, what are the odds of choosing a girl or an A student?

   b. What is the ratio of boys to girls?

   c. What percentage of the class is female?

   d. How many students are not A students?

4. A basket of fruit contains 3 oranges, 2 apples, and 5 bananas.

   a. How many pieces of fruit are in the basket?

   b. How many more bananas are there than oranges?

   c. What is the ratio of oranges to the whole?

   d. If a piece of fruit is chosen at random, what are the odds of getting an orange or a banana?

5. An estimated 43% of drivers wear a seat belt while behind the wheel.

   a. What percentage of drivers do not wear a seat belt?

   b. How many drivers wear a seat belt?

   c. If two people are chosen at random, what is the likelihood that both of them wear a seat belt?

   d. If all the drivers that do not wear a seat belt are given traffic tickets, how many tickets will be written?

6. There are 3 cards chosen from a full deck of cards and they are not replaced.

   a. What is the ratio of cards picked to the number of cards left in the deck?

   b. What percentage of the cards has been removed?

   c. What are the chances of getting a jack, a ten, and a nine?

   d. How many cards are left in the deck?

Area Code

Find the area of each shape. Circle the correct answer, then write the corresponding letter on the lines below to reveal a secret code.

1.

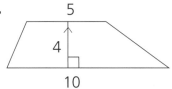

15 F
30 G
60 A

2.

10 E
20 A
5 I

3.

24 I
28 O
26 U

4.

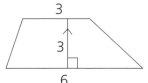

13.5 M
9.5 N
6.5 O

5.

13.5 O
26.5 A
31.5 E

6.

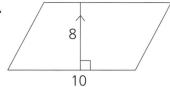

80 T
100 R
40 S

7.

6.5 Q
4.5 R
8.5 S

8.

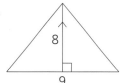

46 Z
63 X
36 Y

9.

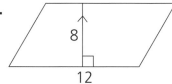

96 F
106 G
48 H

10.

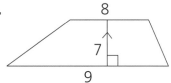

95.5 I
59.0 O
59.5 U

11.

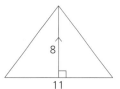

44 N
88 L
66 M

___ ___ ___ ___ ___ ___ ___ ___   ___ ___ ___!
1   2   3   4   5   6   7   8   9   10 11

Birthday Bash

Solve the problems below.

1. Your grandmother's birthday is soon. You want to know how old she will be. You know that she is younger than her sister, who is 88. You also know that your grandmother's age is not an even number, and it is divisible by 3. Your grandma will be more than 3 times as old as your older sister, who is twice your age plus 6. You are 11 years old. How old will your grandmother be on her birthday? _____

2. You are decorating a 2-layer cake for your grandmother's birthday. You want to place flowers along the sides of the bottom layer of the cake, which measures 15 inches × 12 inches. You want to place seashells along the sides of the top layer, which measures 12 inches × 9 inches. Each decoration is 1 inch wide and you need 2 inches between each decoration. The decorations should be symmetrical on opposite sides. How many decorations of each kind do you need? _____

3. You want to get grandma a special present for her birthday. There is a watch you saw in a store that cost $200. You saved your weekly $7 allowance for 16 weeks, mowed 8 of your neighbors' lawns for $6.50 per lawn, and cashed in all the change from your piggy bank. You had 20 quarters, 32 dimes, 49 nickels, and 88 pennies. Your parents said that if you do not have enough money for the watch, you could borrow some from them. Do you have enough money? _____ If not, how much will you need to borrow? _____

4. You want to make sure grandma has the best birthday party. You decorate with 80 balloons. Of the balloons, 30% are red, 25% are purple, 15% are green, and the remainder are yellow. You also buy 60 party hats for the guests. Of the party hats, 20% are orange, 45% are blue, 10% are white, and the remainder are pink. Write how many of each color balloons and hats you bought:

_____ red balloons   _____ orange hats

_____ purple balloons   _____ blue hats

_____ green balloons   _____ white hats

_____ yellow balloons   _____ pink hats

117

Connect the Dots

Perform the graphing activities as follows.

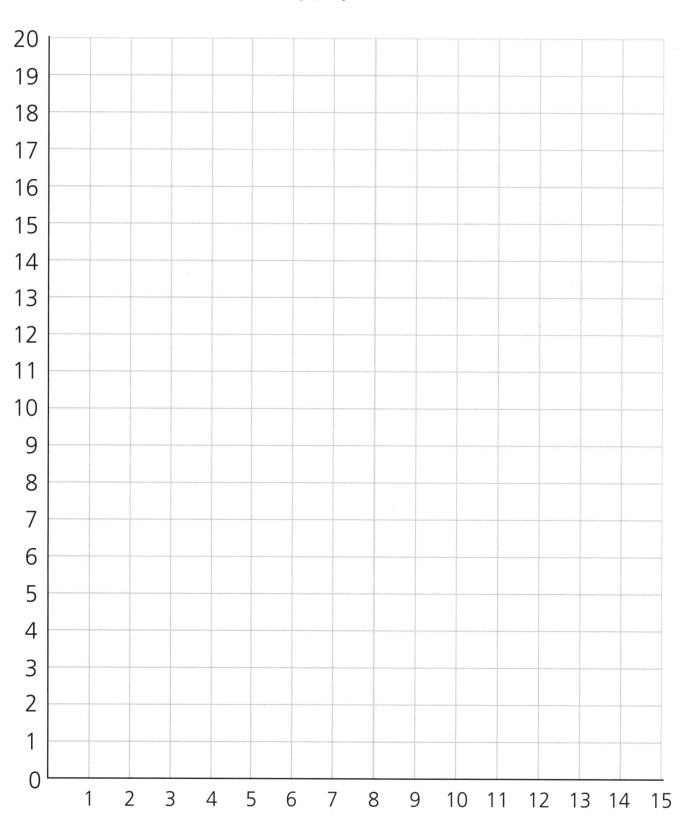

1. Plot the following points on the graph and label each with its corresponding letter.

A (1,7)	I (14,8)	Q (10,4)
B (1,8)	J (14,7)	R (5,4)
C (2,9)	K (13,6)	S (3,2)
D (3,9)	L (13,5)	T (2,2)
E (5,7)	M (14,4)	U (1,3)
F (10,7)	N (14,3)	V (1,4)
G (12,9)	O (13,2)	W (2,5)
H (13,9)	P (12,2)	X (2,6)

2. Connect the points in alphabetical order. What is revealed? _____

3. Plot the following points on the graph and label each with its corresponding letter. Keep them separate from the points already marked.

A (3,18)

B (4,19)

C (5,19)

D (7,17)

E (9,19)

F (10,19)

G (11,18)

H (11,16)

I (7,12)

J (3,16)

4. Connect the points in alphabetical order. What is revealed? _____

Recipe Converter

Using the information in the box, rewrite the recipe using standard measurements, including the instructions. Give your answers in decimal form and round to the nearest hundredth.

5 ml = 1 teaspoon	240 ml = 1 cup	100 grams = 3.5 ounces
15 ml = 1 tablespoon	1 liter = 4.2 cups	$°C = (\frac{9}{5})°F + 32$

METRIC COOKIE RECIPE

550 ml flour

5 ml baking soda

5 ml salt

250 ml butter

175 ml granulated sugar

175 ml brown sugar

5 ml vanilla extract

2 eggs

2 168-gram packages chocolate chips

250 ml chopped nuts

Preheat the oven to 190°C. In small bowl, combine flour, baking soda, and salt; set aside. In large bowl, combine butter, sugar, brown sugar, and vanilla; beat until creamy. Beat in eggs. Gradually add flour mixture; mix well. Stir in chocolate chips and nuts. Bake 8 to 10 minutes.

Elevator Antics

Use the department store directory to solve the problems below. Hint: think of the floors as integers on a number line.

Finkel's Department Store Directory

5 Furniture

4 Men's Clothing

3 Women's Clothing

2 Shoes

1 Handbags / Jewelry

G Ground Level Cafe

-1 Seasonal Items

-2 Home Goods

-3 Childrens Clothing

1. How many floors higher is Men's Clothing than Seasonal Items? _____

2. How many floors below Furniture is Home Goods?

   _____

3. If you have a bite to eat, then ride up two floors, what are you shopping for? _____

4. If you look for a necklace, then a baking dish, how many floors did you travel? _____

5. True or false? Home Goods < Seasonal Items

   _____

6. If you begin at Men's Clothing, travel down five floors, and then up one floor, where are you? _____

7. To go from Furniture to Seasonal Items, how many floors will you travel? _____

8. What is on the floor that is twice the distance that Shoes is from the ground floor? _____

When in Rome

Use the information about Roman numerals in the box below to solve the problems.

I = 1	L = 50	M = 1,000
V = 5	C = 100	
X = 10	D = 500	

Hint: If a smaller character comes after a larger character, add the value of the two characters together. If a smaller character comes before a larger character, subtract the value of the smaller character from the value of the larger character.

1. XI _____

2. XXVI _____

3. IX _____

4. XL _____

5. CLXVII _____

6. LIX _____

7. XLIII   _____

8. XVI   _____

9. XCIX   _____

10. XLIX   _____

11. CCLXVII   _____

12. DCCXVII   _____

13. MMMCCLXXXI   _____

14. Write the current year in Roman numerals. _____

15. Write the year of your birth in Roman numerals. _____

16. Write the year of a parent or sibling's birth in Roman numerals. _____

Altamont Hill

Solve the problems below.

1. Keith, Craig, Jessica, Allison, Larry, and Renee all live on Altamont Hill. Each of their house numbers has three digits, but the only digits in their house numbers are 2, 3, 5, and 6. The same digit appears twice in one of the addresses. Allison's house number is Jessica's house number doubled. Jessica lives next to Larry and directly across the street from Renee. Renee's house number is the lowest on the street. Craig's house number is a higher number than Allison's but has the same three digits as Allison's. Craig and Allison's house numbers both have the same digit in the hundreds place. Keith's house number is the reverse of Jessica's. What is each person's street address? _____

ALTAMONT HILL

_____

_____

2. The house numbers on Altamont Hill get higher as you go farther down the street. The even numbers are on the left as you drive down the street. Use what you learned in the question above to map out the following:

Jessica's house   The location of 260 Altamont Hill

Larry's house   The location of 267 Altamont Hill

Renee's house   The location of 261 Altamont Hill

Mnemonic Devices

Use the following mnemonic devices to answer the questions that follow.

PleaseExcuseMyDearAuntSallyPleaseExcuseMyDearAuntSallyPleaseExcuseMyDear . . .

This mnemonic device allows us to remember the Order of Operations in math.

1. Based on the information provided, what do you think the first letter of each word actually stands for? _____

_____

2. In the pattern of letters, what will be the 100th letter? _____

3. How many letters are there before the 33rd A? _____

MyVeryEarnestMotherJustServedUsNutsMyVeryEarnestMotherJustServedUsNuts . . .

This mnemonic device is a good way to remember the order of the planets.

4. Based on the information provided, what do you think the first letter of each word actually stands for? _____

_____

5. Based on the pattern of letters, how many Os will there be in the first 175 letters? _____

6. How many vowels will there be in the first 140 letters? _____

Alphabet Angles

What type of angle is marked on each letter?

1.

_____

2.

_____

3.

_____

4.

_____

5.

_____

6.

_____

7.

_____

8.

_____

9.

_____

10.

_____

Maintaining Balance

Fill in each blank with a correct weight from the box to create balanced scales.

1.

2.

3.

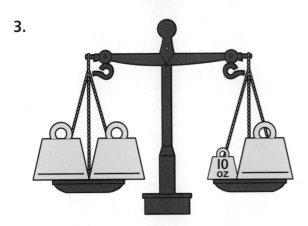

4.

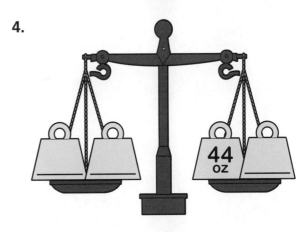

5.

6.

Rock, Paper, Scissors

The game rock, paper, scissors is played between two students: Student 1 and Student 2.
Solve the following probability questions.

Student 1

Student 2

1. How many possible outcomes does the game have? _____

2. Draw a tree diagram to explain your answer.

3. What is the probability that Student 1 will win in any round? _____

4. What is the probability that Student 2 will win in any round? _____

5. Is rock, paper, scissors a fair game? Provide an explanation. _____

_____

6. Who wins the round of rock, paper, scissors in the picture? _____

Tree Diagrams

Solve the probability questions below.

1. A dog biscuit company makes biscuits in three flavors: chicken, beef, and cheese. The biscuits may be either circular or rectangular in shape. Create a tree diagram showing how many different types of biscuits the company makes. Show your work. Write your final answer on the line. _____

2. What are the odds that any random biscuit would be a circle? Express your answer as a percent.

_____

3. What are the odds that any random biscuit will be beef and a rectangle? Express your answer as a fraction. _____

4. The same company makes dog toys in three shapes: bone, hydrant, and newspaper. Each toy can be red, blue, or yellow. Create a tree diagram showing how many different types of toys the company makes. Show your work. Write your final answer on the line. _____

5. If the company makes 90 biscuits, how many will be red or blue? _____

6. The same company starts adding a scent to their toys, which includes spearmint (s), peanut butter (pb), or garlic (g). Create a tree diagram showing how many different types of toys the company would be producing. Show your work. Write your final answer on the line. _____

7. What is the likelihood that you would pick a peanut butter-scented toy at random? Express your answer as a fraction. _____

8. What are the odds that you would pick a red, garlic-scented bone; a blue, peanut butter-scented newspaper; or a yellow, spearmint-scented hydrant at random? _____

Pinheads

In bowling, players generally roll two balls in each frame. The score of each frame is the sum of their two rolls. However, if a player rolls a strike, the score for the frame is 10 points plus the score of his or her next two rolls. If a player gets a spare, the score for that frame is 10 points plus the score of his or her next roll. Note: for purposes of scoring a frame with a strike or a spare in it, additional strikes or spares on subsequent rolls count as 10 points. For each player, add up the score for each frame. Then add the frames together to see the player's score for the game.

KEY	
–	hit no pins
X	strike
/	spare

	Stacy	Maya	Jason	Jack
Frame 1	4 and 2	3 and 5	– and 8	X
Frame 2	– and 9	7 and /	4 and /	X
Frame 3	X	7 and –	X	8 and /
Frame 4	6 and /	5 and /	1 and 7	X
Frame 5	8 and 1	6 and 2	3 and 5	7 and 2
Frame 6	X	6 and /	X	9 and –
Frame 7	– and 7	– and –	2 and /	X
Frame 8	6 and 3	8 and 1	X	X
Frame 9	4 and /	7 and 2	X	X
Frame 10	8 and –	8 and 1	8 and 1	2 and /

	Stacy	Maya	Jason	Jack
Frame 1				
Frame 2				
Frame 3				
Frame 4				
Frame 5				
Frame 6				
Frame 7				
Frame 8				
Frame 9				
Frame 10				
Total				

1. Who won the game? _____

2. How many points separated the winner from the second-place bowler? _____

3. Who lost the game? _____

Jargon Game

Draw a line to connect the mathematical term to its definition.

sum

expression

evaluate

difference

variable

identity property of addition

Substitute given values for the variables and perform the operations to find the value of the expression.

The result of subtraction.

A number, variable, or combination of numbers, variables, and operation signs.

The sum of any number and 0 is that number.

The answer to an addition problem.

A letter or symbol that represents a number in an algebraic expression.

131

Relating

Use the pictures to solve the problems below.

Matthew	Danielle	David	Martha
Age 8	Age 15	Age 17	Age 12
80 pounds	110 pounds	180 pounds	100 pounds
Shoe size 2	Shoe size 8	Shoe size 11	Shoe size 6

1. Martha is 4 years less than twice the age of her cousin. Who is her cousin?

_____

2. Matthew weighs 10 pounds less than $\frac{1}{2}$ the weight of his sibling. Who is his sibling?

_____

3. Danielle's shoe size is 5 more than $\frac{1}{2}$ of her sibling. Who is her sibling? _____

4. Whose weights are represented by the ratio 4:9? _____

5. Whose weights are represented by the ratio 10:11? _____

6. How is David related to Danielle? _____

Mixed Brainteasers

Use the information in each problem to solve the brainteaser.

1. You empty your piggy bank to reveal 16 coins. You have the same number of nickels as pennies, $1.00 in quarters, and 2 more dimes than quarters. How much money do you have?

_____

2. Your watch is broken! Sometimes the hands move in the reverse direction. Yesterday, it read a quarter to 10. It ran backward for 14 hours and 6 minutes. Then, it ran forward again for 5 hours and 53 minutes. Finally, the clock ran backward for 10 hours and 41 minutes. What time will the watch show now? _____

3. You received $0.20 change from a $5.00 bill when you bought tomatoes, green peppers, and cucumbers at a farm stand. Tomatoes cost $1.50 per pound. Green peppers cost $0.40 each. Cucumbers cost $0.30 each. You bought 4 tomatoes, which weighed 2 pounds altogether. If you bought 1 fewer green pepper than tomatoes, how many cucumbers did you buy?

_____

4. Your cousin Marion is twice your age. Your brother is two years older than Marion. Your brother is $\frac{1}{3}$ the age of your aunt. Your aunt has been alive $\frac{1}{2}$ as many years as your 72-year-old grandmother. How old are you? _____

5. Jim and Rita have saved $34.88 total to buy supplies for their new cat. They bought 18 cans of food for $15.48. They bought 2 bags of litter for $2.86 each. Toys cost $3.89, and a carrier cost $7.21. With the money they have left, how many extra cans of food would they be able to buy? _____

Time Table

Use the table to solve the problems.

Time Units	In this Time Unit
60 seconds	minute
60 minutes	hour
24 hours	day
7 days	week
about 30 days	month
365 days	normal year
366 days	leap year
12 months	year
52 weeks	year
10 years	decade
20 years	score
100 years	century
1,000 years	millennium

1. How many hours are there in 1 week? _____

2. How many seconds are there in 1 day? _____

3. How many minutes are there in 1 week? _____

4. How many hours are there in a leap year? _____

5. How many months are there in a century? _____

6. How many weeks are there in a decade? _____

7. How many minutes are there in 1 year? _____

8. How many days are there in a millennium if there are 250 leap years during that time?

_____

9. How many weeks are there in a score? _____

10. How many minutes are there in a 31-day month? _____

Garden Games

Use the information below to solve the problems.

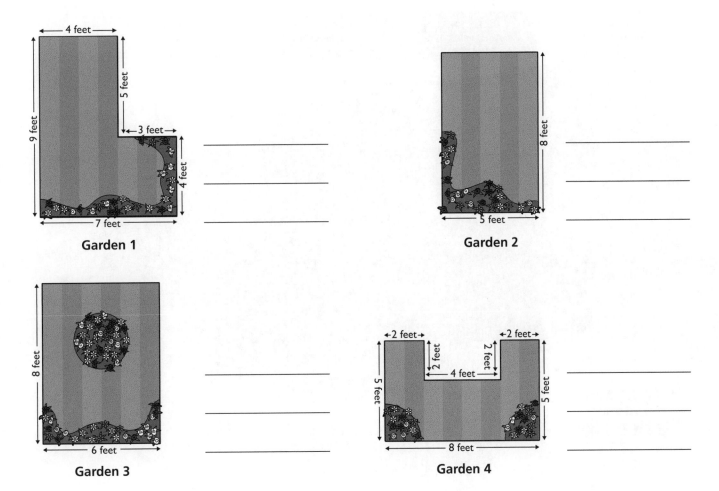

Garden 1

Garden 2

Garden 3

Garden 4

Brian, Jonah, Stewart, and Rosa are planting flowers in their gardens. The areas of Brian's and Jonah's gardens are the same, but the perimeter of Brian's garden is greater than Jonah's. The actual number of feet in the perimeter of Brian's garden is equal to the number of square feet in Rosa's garden. The perimeter of Rosa's garden is greater than the perimeter of Stewart's garden. The area of Stewart's garden is less than the area of Jonah's garden.

1. Which garden belongs to each gardener? Write the person's name next to the garden that belongs to him or her.

2. What is the perimeter of each garden? Write it under the name of the person whose garden it is.

3. What is the area of each person's garden? Write it under the perimeter of each garden.

What Time Is It?

Use the map to solve the problems.

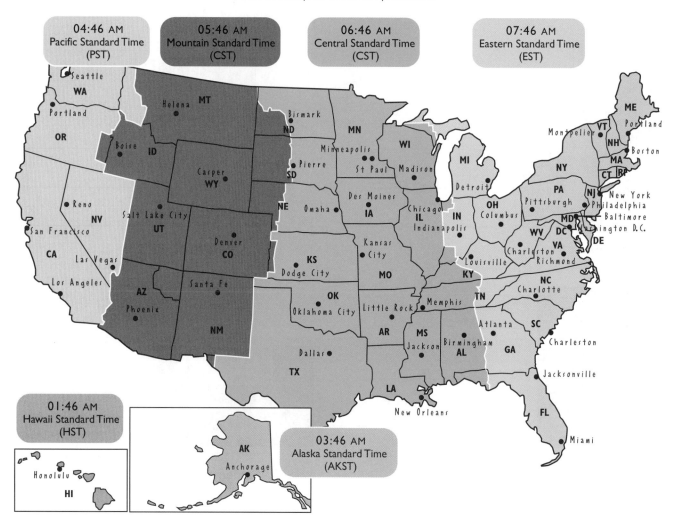

The world is broken up into 24 geographic areas for the purpose of maintaining a standard time system. Clocks within a given time zone are set to the same time, which is generally one hour later than the zone immediately to the west.

1. In which time zone is San Francisco, California? _____

2. In which time zone is Anchorage, Alaska? _____

3. Name one state in the Eastern Standard Time Zone. _____

4. Name one state in the Mountain Standard Time Zone. _____

5. If it is 5 PM in New York City, what time is it in Dallas, Texas? _____

6. If it is 6 AM in Seattle, Washington, what time is it in New Orleans, Louisiana? _____

My Weight

Develop your own unit of weight! Choose any small object around the house, such as a calculator, cell phone, banana, or fork.

What did you choose? My unit of weight is a _____.

Now, weigh your object. One _____ weighs _____ ounces.

Now, use your object to determine the weight of other things around your house.
Do this ten times. Record your findings here.

Object	Weight in My Units	True Weight (Indicate Measure)
1.		
2.		
3.		
4.		
5.		
6.		
7.		
8.		
9.		
10.		

Parking Puzzle

Use the information in the problem to find the coordinates for each car's parking space.
Mark the family's name and their coordinates on the graph.

The Smith family parked their car in the first spot in the first row: spot (1,1). The Bright family parked their car in the first row, 4 spots to the right of the Smiths' car. The Willises' car is halfway between the Smiths' car and the Brights' car, but 3 spots closer to the store. The Costners' car is in the same row as the Willises' car, but 2 spots closer to the street. The Quigleys' car is five spots above the street entrance. And the Higginses' car is 2 spots to the right of that.

Algebra Quiz!

Use algebra to solve the problems below.

1. Rita walks 10 dogs. She walks 4 times as many poodles as beagles. How many poodles does Rita walk?

   a. 8

   b. 4

   c. 10

   d. 40

2. If $n = 6$ in the equation below, what belongs on the blank line?

$$5n \underline{\hspace{1cm}} 6n - 4$$

   a. $>$

   b. $<$

   c. $=$

   d. none of the above

3. You purchase two goldfish and one can of fish food for $5.00. A can of food costs $3.00. What is the price of each fish?

   a. $4

   b. $1

   c. $3

   d. $2

4. Solve for x in the equation below.

$$\frac{6}{7} = \frac{42}{x}$$

   a. 42

   b. 7

   c. 49

   d. 21

5. Choose the rule for the function table.

x	y
1	6
2	7
3	8

   a. $y = 5x$

   b. $y = x + 5$

   c. $y = x - 5$

   d. $y = 5 - x$

6. In Paulo's pencil box there are pencils, markers, and crayons. There are 5 fewer markers than pencils. There are 8 pencils. There are 22 writing utensils in all. How many crayons are there?

   a. 11

   b. 8

   c. 3

   d. 9

Equation Matters

For each problem, choose the equation that would find a solution.

1. The chef at Cielo cooked 18 mini quiches. Mary ate 2 less than $\frac{1}{2}$ of them. How many mini quiches did Mary eat?

   a. $q = 18 \times 2 - 2$
   b. $182 + \frac{1}{2} = q$
   c. $q = 18 \div 2 - 2$

2. To make his famous macaroni and cheese, the chef at Cielo used $\frac{1}{2}$ box of pasta. $1\frac{3}{4}$ boxes of pasta were left. How many boxes of pasta were there to begin with?

   a. $1\frac{3}{4} + \frac{1}{2} = p$
   b. $p = 1\frac{3}{4} - \frac{1}{2}$
   c. $1\frac{3}{4} + p = \frac{1}{2}$

3. In the last three nights, 24 candles were burned on the tables at Cielo. On Tuesday, 4 more candles were burned than on Monday. On Wednesday, 3 times as many candles were burned as on Monday. How many candles were burned on Monday?

   a. $24 = 4(3 + 4)$
   b. $c + (c + 4) + 3c = 24$
   c. $24 - 4 - 3 = c$

4. The patrons at Cielo ate 73 dinner rolls from 4 batches. From the first batch, 23 rolls were eaten. From the second batch, 6 rolls were eaten. From the third batch, 18 rolls were eaten. How many dinner rolls from the fourth batch were eaten?

   a. $73 - 4 - 23 - 6 - 18 = f$
   b. $f = 23 + 6 + 18$
   c. $23 + 6 + 18 + f = 73$

5. The waitstaff at Cielo was clumsy tonight. Emily dropped 2 glasses, David dropped 4 glasses, and Eva dropped 3 glasses. Ryan dropped 4 times as many glasses as the other waitstaff combined. How many glasses did Ryan drop?

   a. $2 \times 4 \times 3 = g$
   b. $g = 4(2 + 4 + 3)$
   c. $g = 2 + 4 + 3 + 4$

6. The chef at Cielo loves his own food! He ate 6 mini quiches on Tuesday and 3 fewer on Wednesday. He ate 4 times as many on Monday as on Tuesday. How many mini quiches did the chef eat?

   a. $q = 6 + 3 + 4$
   b. $q = 6 + (6 - 3) + (4 \times 6)$
   c. $4(6 - 3) + 6 = q$

On the Menu

At Bistro Daniel, there are a number of combinations that can be chosen from their multicourse menu. Look at the menu below. Then, in the box at the bottom of the page, create tree diagrams to demonstrate how many different dinner combinations you can make if you pick one entrée, one side, and one dessert. Use a separate sheet of paper if needed.

Treasure Map

Use the map to solve the problems.

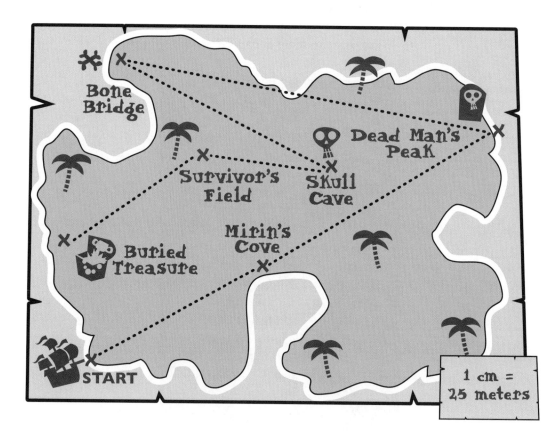

1. Using a ruler, measure the distances between points (in centimeters). Mark your answers on the map.

2. What is the actual distance between Mirin's Cove and Dead Man's Peak? _____

3. What is the actual distance between Bone Bridge and Skull Cave? _____

4. What is the actual distance between Survivor's Field and the Buried Treasure? _____

5. If you travel from the Start to Mirin's Cove to Dead Man's Peak, how far will you have gone?

   _____

6. The shore of the Caribbean Sea is 275 meters from the Start. If you draw a line from the Start to the sea, how many centimeters long would it have to be? _____

My Room

Choose a room in your home and measure its dimensions using a tape measure. Then solve the problems below.

What are the dimensions of the room? _____

What is the square footage of the room? _____

What is the area of the room? _____

What is the perimeter of the room? _____

Now determine the scale of the room in order to draw it below.

Scale: _____ = 1 square foot

Use the space here to make a scale drawing of the room. Mark doorways and windows.

More Mixed Brainteasers

Answer the following brainteasers.

Item	Price
T-shirt	$10.00
hat	$7.50
sports bottle	$4.75
car banner	$3.50

1. The Crusaders hockey team had a team fund-raiser at which they raised $476.25 by selling various items. They sold $115.50 worth of car banners. The amount collected for hats was $3.00 less than the amount collected for the car banners. The amount of money collected for T-shirts was $7.50 more than the amount of money collected for hats. How many of each item was sold at the fund-raiser?

_____

_____

_____

_____

2. There are 8 students taking horseback-riding lessons together. The students are 7, 9, and 10 years old. The mode of their current ages is 10, and the mean of their current ages is 9. There are an equal number of students that are 7 years old and 9 years old. Next year, the class will resume at the same time of year with the same students. How many students of each age will there be in the class next year? _____

_____

3. Every Thursday in January held a record-low temperature for the date. On Thursday, January 30, the low was 5°F. This was 7 degrees more than the low temperature on the Thursday prior. The low temperature on Thursday, January 9, was 2 degrees lower than the low on Thursday, January 16. On the first Thursday of the month, the low temperature was 3 degrees lower than the low on January 23. The low temperature on the Thursday in the middle of January was 6 degrees higher than the low temperature on the first Thursday of January. What was the low temperature for each Thursday in January?

_____

_____

_____

_____

Mary Loves Ice Cream

Answer the following logic questions about Mary.

1. Mary has an ice cream cone with 5 scoops of ice cream. Each of Mary's 5 scoops of ice cream is a different flavor. The five flavors are mint chip, chocolate, strawberry, vanilla, and pistachio. The vanilla scoop touches both the chocolate and pistachio scoops. The bottom flavor has 10 letters. The vanilla scoop is below the chocolate scoop but above the mint chip scoop. Determine what order the ice cream flavors are in on Mary's cone, from the top of the cone to the bottom.

_____

_____

_____

_____

_____

2. Mary's mother has four kids. The first child is named Margo. The second daughter is named Madge. The third child is named Michaela. What is the name of the fourth child?

_____

3. Mary went to dinner with four of her friends: Abby, Christopher, Cadyn, and Tarek. They each ordered a different meal, but when the waiter brought the plates of food, he put them down in front of the wrong people. Abby disliked the slice of meat lasagna in front of her. Christopher hated the cheeseburger in front of him, as well as any other food with cheese on it. Cadyn disliked the steak in front of him because he doesn't eat meat. Mary pushed away her shrimp because she is allergic to seafood. Seafood is the one item on the table that Tarek likes, but he was served a vegetable plate. What did Mary order? _____

4. Mary went to see her neighbors, the Whitmans, this evening. The group ordered two large pizzas. Each pizza had six slices. One of the pizzas had mushrooms on the whole thing and onions on half. The other pizza had green peppers and onion on half and sausage on the other half. Brian Whitman ate two slices with mushroom and onion. He hates green peppers. Ben Whitman ate two slices with just mushrooms. He is allergic to all of the other toppings. Boden Whitman ate two slices with onions and green peppers. He dislikes sausage. Beverly Whitman ate two slices with sausage. She dislikes onions and mushrooms. Mary ate two slices that did not have onion on them because she hates onions. There were two slices of pizza left in the boxes. One hour later, Brian Whitman dug back into the pizza boxes to get seconds, but the two leftover slices were gone! Which person took both of the remaining slices of pizza?

_____

Why That Shape?

Things in your everyday life often have a practical reason for being a certain shape.

CITY SEWER

1. The manhole pictured here is round with a round cover. Why isn't the manhole a rectangle?

_____

_____

_____

_____

2.

Would either of the shapes above make a good manhole cover? _____

Why or why not? _____

_____

3. Would a triangle make a good shape for a manhole cover? _____
Try this: cut a triangle from a piece of cardboard and see if it can easily fall through the hole
formed where you cut it out. Try it with different types of triangles.

Angularity

Perform the following activities related to angles.

1.

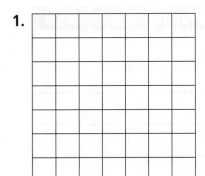

Draw two rays meeting at a point. Name the vertex and measure the angle. Label your angle.

2. A normal intersection forms what type of intersecting lines?

    a. zigzag lines

    b. perpendicular lines

    c. parallel lines

    d. straight lines

3. What type of angle is formed when perpendicular lines intersect?

    a. straight

    b. right

    c. obtuse

    d. acute

4. What type of angles are greater than right angles?

    a. obtuse

    b. acute

    c. right

    d. straight

5. If angle EFG measures 54 degrees, what type of an angle is it?

    a. right

    b. acute

    c. obtuse

    d. straight

6. What are lines that do not cross over one another called? _____
If you measured one of these, how many degrees would its angle be?

_____

Rainy Day Fun

Use the chart to solve the problems below. Round your answers to the nearest hundredth.

	January Rainfall (in inches)	July Rainfall (in inches)
Fort Lauderdale, Florida	2.01	5.7
Seattle, Washington	5.38	0.76
San Francisco, California	4.35	0.03
East Blue Hill, Maine	3.53	3.09
Chicago, Illinois	1.53	3.66
Austin, Texas	1.83	2.31

Adam, Marsha, George, Donna, Edward, and Rachel researched the average rainfall for January and July for the cities in which each of them lives. Adam's city has more rainfall in January than July. Donna's city receives $\frac{3}{10}$ of an inch more rain in January than Edward's city does. Rachel's city gets 3.69 inches more rain in July than in January. The January rainfall in Marsha's city is 2 inches more than the rainfall in Edward's city. There is less than 0.5 inch of rain in July where George lives.

1. In what city does each person live?

_____   _____

_____   _____

_____   _____

2. What is the mean rainfall for January? _____ What is the mean rainfall for July? _____

3. Which city was the rainiest in the two months on the chart? _____

Which city was the driest? _____

4. Which city had the smallest difference in rainfall amounts in the months shown on the chart?

_____

What does this tell you about the weather there? _____

_____

Bake Sale

Use the information below to solve these tasty problems.

PUMPKIN   APPLE   KEY LIME   PEACH

Patty Pie Lover made four different pies for the annual bake sale: pumpkin, apple, key lime, and peach. Each pie was the same size. Patty cut the pumpkin pie into 6 equal slices, the apple pie into 5 equal slices, the key lime pie into 3 equal slices, and the peach pie into 4 equal slices. Avery, Dillon, Liam, and Sierra each bought one slice of pie but ate only a portion of that slice. Each chose a different kind of pie. Avery bought the largest slice available and ate $\frac{1}{4}$ of it. Dillon bought the smallest slice available and ate $\frac{3}{4}$ of it. The slice Liam bought was bigger than the slice Sierra bought. Liam ate $\frac{1}{2}$ of his slice. Sierra ate $\frac{2}{3}$ of her slice.

1. Use a marker to divide the pies pictured above the same way that Patty cut them.

2. What kind of pie did each person choose?

Avery _____   Liam _____

Dillon _____   Sierra _____

3. What fraction of the total pie did each person eat? Reduce your answers to lowest terms.

Avery _____   Liam _____

Dillon _____   Sierra _____

Sailing Away

Look at the sails below and determine the area of each.

1.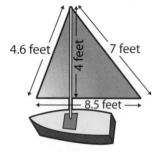

4.6 feet · 4 feet · 7 feet · 8.5 feet

_____

2.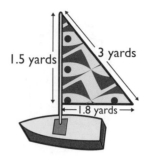

1.5 yards · 3 yards · 1.8 yards

_____

3.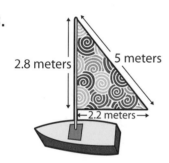

2.8 meters · 5 meters · 2.2 meters

_____

4.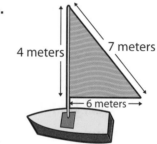

4 meters · 7 meters · 6 meters

_____

5.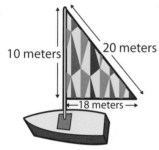

10 meters · 20 meters · 18 meters

_____

6.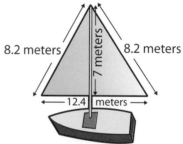

8.2 meters · 7 meters · 8.2 meters · 12.4 meters

_____

7.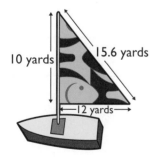

10 yards · 15.6 yards · 12 yards

_____

8.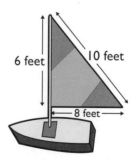

6 feet · 10 feet · 8 feet

_____

Postal Problems

The U.S. Postal Service is always changing the price of stamps.
Use the information in each problem to answer the questions below.

1. You find some old rolls of stamps. One roll has $0.15 stamps, and the other roll has $0.33 stamps. Can you use a combination of these old stamps to mail a package for which shipping costs $1.77? _____

If so, in what combination? _____

2. With the same rolls of stamps as above, can you mail a package that costs $4.77 to ship?

_____

If so, in what combination? _____

3. How about a package that costs $17.76 to ship? Can you mail it with the same rolls of stamps as above? _____

If so, in what combination? _____

4. The price of a stamp changed twice in 1981. First it rose to $0.18 in March and then it rose again to $0.20 in November. What percent was the increase between March and November?

_____

Plot the Path

Use the information and the blank graph below to solve the problems.

Heather began her walk to a friend's house at 2:45 PM. For every 5 minutes she walked, Heather traveled north 2 blocks and east 1 block. She started on the corner of C Street and 2nd Avenue. Heather arrived at her friend's house at 3:10 PM. Heather spent 2 hours and 20 minutes at her friend's house. When she left, she walked a different direction to the store at the corner of K and 6th Streets at the same rate as her earlier walk. Heather spent 10 minutes at the store before walking home.

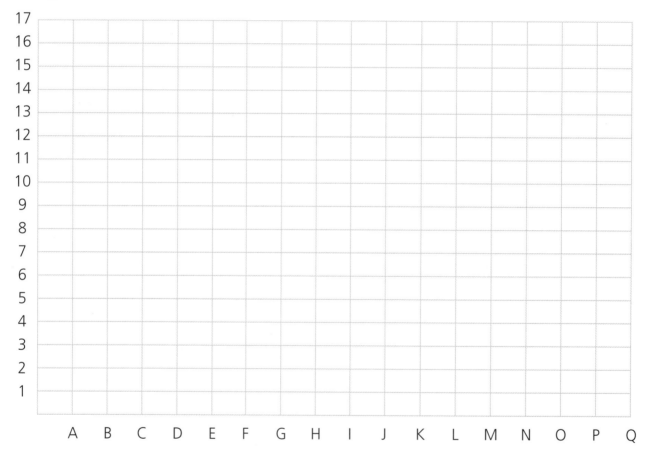

1. Plot out Heather's path to her friend's house, the store, and then home again.

2. On the corner of which streets does Heather's friend live? _____

3. If Heather walked home at the same rate as her other walks, at what time did she get home?

_____

What's Your Combination?

Solve the problems below.

1. If a combination lock requires a code of three numbers from 0 to 39, how many combinations are there? (Numbers can appear more than once.) _____

2. If you are using the same combination lock, but each number can only be used once, how many combinations are there? _____

3. The combination for a lock is 8-31-24. To open the lock, you can also use the numbers directly to the right or left of each number in the combination. How many different combinations will open the lock? _____

4. In recent years, New York City had to add a new area code to its phone coverage region. Why do you think this happened? _____

_____

Beauty Checkout

Determine the subtotal, tax (at 7%), tip (at 20%), and the grand total for each person's services.

1. Eliza

Manicure	$22.00
Pedicure	$35.00
Subtotal	_____
Tax	_____
Tip (before tax)	_____
Total	_____

2. Kerrie

Pedicure	$35.00
Eyebrow wax	$13.00
Subtotal	_____
Tax	_____
Tip (before tax)	_____
Total	_____

3. Hanna

Facial	$75.00
Massage	$90.00
Subtotal	_____
Tax	_____
Tip (before tax)	_____
Total	_____

4. Danielle

French manicure	$27.00
French pedicure	$40.00
Eyebrow wax	$13.00
Subtotal	_____
Tax	_____
Tip (before tax)	_____
Total	_____

5. Sierra

Massage	$90.00
Manicure	$22.00
Subtotal	_____
Tax	_____
Tip (before tax)	_____
Total	_____

6. Morgan

Hot stone massage	$110.00
Pedicure	$35.00
Eyebrow wax	$13.00
Subtotal	_____
Tax	_____
Tip (before tax)	_____
Total	_____

7. Marianne

French manicure	$27.00
French pedicure	$40.00
Subtotal	_____
Tax	_____
Tip (before tax)	_____
Total	_____

8. Shannon

Manicure	$22.00
Pedicure	$35.00
Massage	$90.00
Subtotal	_____
Tax	_____
Tip (before tax)	_____
Total	_____

Exponent Exercises

Draw a line to match the exponential number to its value.

13^2	512
6^1	1,296
5^4	169
6^4	6
8^3	625

Now determine the value of each expression.

1. 100^3 _____

2. $4^2 \times 10^2$ _____

3. $9^2 \times 2^2 \times 3^2$ _____

4. $5 \times 6^3 \times 10^3$ _____

5. $10 \times 4 \times 6^2$ _____

6. $5^2 \times 8^2 \times 3^3$ _____

Pump Up the Volume

Solve the following problems related to volume.

1. Take a sheet $8\frac{1}{2}$" × 11" notebook or printer paper and roll it up so that the long sides meet. Now take a second sheet of $8\frac{1}{2}$" × 11" paper and roll it up so that the short sides meet. Does one of these cylinders hold more, or have a larger volume, than the other? Provide an explanation.

_____

_____

_____

2. What size paper could you use in this experiment and always get the same volume cylinder?

_____

3. Take two equal lengths of wire and bend each into the shape of a rectangle. Will they have the same area? _____

_____

4. Look in your pantry or at the grocery store. Find two different-shaped containers that hold the exact same amount. What are the contents of each? _____

_____

Pick the Measure

Circle the correct measurement in each sentence.

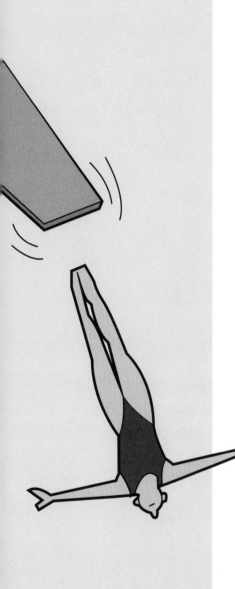

1. A gymnastic balance beam is only 4 (inches, feet, yards) wide.

2. Boxers get just 60 (seconds, minutes, days) between rounds of a fight.

3. A diving platform is an amazing 33 (inches, feet, yards) high.

4. A high jump bar can be as high as 7 (inches, yards, feet) in the air.

5. Baseballs are often pitched as fast as fast as 90 (inches, feet, miles) per hour.

6. A softball weighs about 7 (pounds, ounces, tons).

7. A basketball net stands about 10 (feet, yards, inches) off the ground.

8. A soccer game is generally 90 (minutes, seconds, days) in duration.

9. A standard hockey puck weighs about $5\frac{1}{2}$ (ounces, pounds, tons).

10. A regulation basketball is $29\frac{1}{2}$ (yards, feet, inches) in diameter.

Division Message

Determine the quotient for each long division problem. Match each quotient in the hidden message below to a letter to reveal a message. Then look up the message in the dictionary and write its definition below.

1. $7\overline{)630}$ C

2. $24\overline{)720}$ I

3. $41\overline{)902}$ L

4. $53\overline{)424}$ N

5. $31\overline{)899}$ O

6. $24\overline{)744}$ V

7. $91\overline{)819}$ E

8. $65\overline{)780}$ A

9. $12\overline{)7,584}$ T

10. $41\overline{)31,734}$ D

| ___ | ___ | ___ | ___ | ___ | ___ | ___ | ___ | ___ | ___ | ___ |
| 90 | 29 | 8 | 632 | 30 | 8 | 9 | 8 | 632 | 12 | 22 |

| ___ | ___ | ___ | ___ | ___ | ___ |
| 774 | 30 | 31 | 30 | 774 | 9 |

_____

_____

_____

Categorization Crunch

This table shows the prices for basic items at five different grocery stores. Use it to solve the problems below.

Store	Bread	Milk	Eggs	Coffee	Orange Juice
A	$0.89	$1.90	$1.79	$5.99	$2.39
B	$1.19	$1.65	$1.75	$6.24	$2.49
C	$1.09	$1.99	$1.65	$5.33	$3.24
D	$1.49	$1.75	$2.05	$5.88	$2.75
E	$0.99	$1.89	$2.13	$6.12	$2.33

1. Which two stores have the most similar prices? _____

2. Which two stores have the largest difference in their prices? _____

3. Now look in your own cabinets. Which of the cereals in your cupboard are most alike? Provide an explanation of how they are alike. Consider the price, taste, size, and appearance.

_____

_____

_____

4. Now look at the shoes in your closet. Identify three characteristics that can be used to describe your shoes.

_____

_____

_____

5. Categorize your shoes according to the characteristics you named in question 4. Which pairs of shoes are most alike? Provide an explanation.

_____

_____

_____

Jon's Porch

Use the information below to solve the problems.

Jon is designing a porch for his house. It will be in the shape of a trapezoid. Jon has labeled the four corners A, B, C, and D. Line BC is 20 feet long and runs along the living room. Line AB is 8 feet long and is perpendicular to line BC. Line CD is parallel to line AB but is twice as long as line AB. Line AD represents the longest wall with the most windows. Line AE is an imaginary line parallel to line BC. Point E is on line CD and is the midpoint of line CD.

1. Use the blank space to draw the deck. Label its points and dimensions.

2. Jon wants to lay tiles on the floor of the porch. The tiles are 12 square inches each, and the tiles come in boxes of a dozen. Jon needs to order an additional two dozen tiles to make sure he has enough in the event he breaks any. How many boxes of floor tiles should Jon order? _____

Through the Trees

Solve for each equation. Check your answers by finding them among the trees.

1. $2t + 6 = 22$

2. $64 = 8(x - 5)$

3. $(5 + n)22 = 132$

4. $31 = 8q - 9$

5. $91 = \dfrac{b + 6}{2}$

6. $9 + 12p = 81$

7. $4g + g - 2g + 3 = 54$

8. $134 = 7y - 10 + 5y$

9. $3x + 22 - x = 44$

10. What numbers hiding in the trees are *not* answers to the questions above? Circle them.

On Sale

Use estimation to solve the problems.

1. You are the last person in a line of 299 others. You are all waiting to purchase tickets for a concert. How could you figure out how long it will take you to get your ticket?

_____

_____

_____

_____

2. If you are standing in the same line and you are still in the same spot, about how many feet away from the ticket window are you? How could you determine this?

_____

_____

_____

3. There are 600 tickets available for the concert. The ticket window opens 30 minutes prior to the start of the concert. How many ticket windows should there be to accommodate all 600 people before the show starts? How could you answer this?

_____

_____

_____

4. Go to the grocery store with an adult and note the following:

What is the mean number of people standing in each line? _____

What is the mean amount of time it takes them to get to the checker? _____

From doing this experiment, did you find that the express line was truly faster than the others?

_____

MacBurger

Use the information provided to answer each question below.

MacBurger Menu

Hamburger $2.25

French Fries $0.95

Onion Rings $1.25

Soda $0.50

Milk $1.00

Coffee $0.75

Ice Cream $1.50

1. What is the average cost of a beverage at MacBurger?

_____

2. What is the cost of 125 orders of french fries at MacBurger?

_____

3. The following people are on line at MacBurger: Josh, Wendy, Gabe, Baron, and Andy. Josh is ahead of Wendy, but behind Gabe. There are three people between Gabe and Baron. Andy is behind Josh, but ahead of Wendy. In what order is everyone standing? _____

_____

4. You are waiting to place an order at MacBurger when 11 coins totaling $1.37 fall out of your pocket. What are these coins?

_____

5. What items from the menu can you get with the amount of money that fell out of your pocket? _____

_____

_____

6. Once a month, MacBurger offers a special deal to sports teams. When a coach brings in his or her entire team, hamburgers are buy 5, get 1 free for players! This month, the Wizards team went to MacBurger for lunch after its game. Each person had one hamburger. Each of the players had a soda and shared an order of french fries with one other teammate. The two coaches each had their own french fries and coffee. The total bill came to $42.10. How many players are on the Wizards? _____

Olympic Calls

The Olympic athletes could call home to the United States from China for the rates indicated in the chart.
Use the chart to solve the problems that follow.

City Called	Cost Per Minute on Weekdays		Cost Per Minute on Weekends and Holidays
	7 AM to 9 PM	9 PM to 7 AM	All Day
Los Angeles	$3.60	$0.79	$0.45
New York	$2.90	$0.87	$0.30
Atlanta	$1.98	$0.55	$0.15
Kansas City	$2.10	$0.45	$0.10
Detroit	$3.15	$0.70	$0.25
Houston	$3.30	$0.65	$0.20
Santa Fe	$2.00	$0.50	$0.05

1. Track star Tim called Atlanta at 12 PM on a Sunday. The call was 9 minutes long. How much did it cost? _____

2. Golfer Greg called Houston on a Wednesday at 3 PM and spoke for 35 minutes. Then he called New York immediately after and spoke for 22 minutes. At what time did he finish his call to New York? _____ How much did his calls cost altogether? _____

3. Biker Ben made a 20-minute call to Detroit on a Thursday at 8:45 PM. How much did his call cost? _____

4. Diver Doreen made a 20-minute call to New York that cost $6.00. When did she call? _____

5. Equestrian Edna had $23.75 to spend on a phone call. How long could she talk to her mom in Los Angeles after 9 PM on a Monday? _____

6. Gymnast Gerry made a call that cost $36.00 and was placed to Santa Fe at 11 AM on a Tuesday. How long was the call? _____

Finish Line

Solve the problems.

1. Jack and Diane are running a 50-meter race against each other. When Diane crossed the finish line, Jack was at the 45-meter mark. Jack and Diane race again, but Jack starts 5 meters ahead of Diane. They run at the same pace as they did in their first race. Who wins this time?

_____

2. Jack and Diane are running laps around a 50-meter track. Diane runs at the same pace as her previous races against Jack. After how many laps will Diane be one entire lap ahead of Jack?

_____

3. If Jack and Diane start running toward each other from opposite ends of the 50-meter track, where will they meet? _____

4. Determine the order in which the runners finished the race: Tom is behind Tim. Tristan is ahead of Tim. Troy is ahead of Tom. Tom is four runners behind Trevor. _____

_____

5. Determine the order in which the runners finished the race: Mike and Malcolm are ahead of Andres. Mike is behind Andrew and ahead of Karima. Kevin is ahead of Mike and there are two runners between them. There are three runners between Karima and Kevin. Malcolm is ahead of Mike but behind Andrew. _____

_____

Bull's-Eye

Use the archery board to solve the problems that follow.

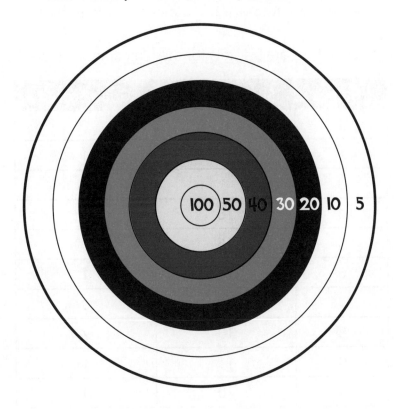

100 50 40 30 20 10 5

1. During Paige's practice yesterday, 40% of her 55 shots hit the 50-point ring. How many of Paige's shots hit the 50-point ring? _____

2. In Max's practice yesterday, he hit the bull's-eye 20% of the time, which was 27 times. How many times did Max shoot altogether? _____

3. In Max's first round, he shot 4 bull's-eyes out of 22 shots he took altogether. What percentage of Max's shots were bull's-eyes? _____

4. In her first round, Lauren scored 165 points. She shot 6 arrows. What percent of total possible points did Lauren score in that round? _____

5. In her second round, Lauren hit the bull's-eye once, the 50-point ring twice, the 40-point ring three times, the 30-point ring twice, and the 10-point ring twice. How many points did she score altogether in this round? _____

6. In the previous question, what percentage of Lauren's points was scored by hitting the 10- and 30-point rings combined? _____

Game Stats

Jeffrey and Bethany are their school's best soccer players.
Use the stats sheets for each player to solve the problems that follow.

Jeffrey plays goalkeeper. Here are his stats for the ten games he played in this season.

Game	Shots on Goal	Goals Scored
1	8	0
2	12	1
3	9	2
4	18	3
5	16	0
6	7	1
7	10	0
8	15	2
9	11	1
10	20	4

1. How many goals were scored against Jeffrey? _____

2. How many shots on goal did Jeffrey successfully block? _____

3. Write the ratio of goals scored to total shots attempted on goal. Reduce your answer to lowest terms. _____

4. How many goals did Jeffrey block in games 5 through 10? _____

5. What percentage of goals did Jeffrey block in all 10 games combined? _____

6. What was the difference between the number of attempted shots on goal and the number of goals scored in the tenth game? _____

7. What were Jeffrey's three best games in terms of ratio of blocked shots to attempted shots on goal? _____

8. What was Jeffrey's worst game in terms of ratio of blocked shots to attempted shots on goal?

_____

Bethany plays forward. Here are her stats for the ten games she played this season.

Game	Attempts	Goals
1	8	2
2	4	0
3	9	2
4	11	3
5	12	3
6	5	1
7	7	2
8	13	4
9	5	1
10	8	1

9. How many goals did Bethany score in these 10 games combined? _____

10. How many shots on goal did Bethany attempt in these 10 games combined? _____

11. What was Bethany's ratio of goals scored to attempted shots on goal? _____

12. What percentage of Bethany's shots ended in goals in game 8? _____

13. Which game was Bethany's best in terms of the ratio of goals made to attempted shots on goal? _____

14. Which two games had the greatest difference between attempts on goal and goals scored?

_____

15. How many of Bethany's attempts on goal were unsuccessful in these 10 games combined?

_____

16. Which two games were Bethany's worst in terms of the ratio of goals to attempts on goal?

_____

OOO Tic-Tac-Toe

Use order of operations (OOO) to perform the activity below.

1. Begin by solving the problems in the grid, and remember to use order of operations!

2. Think of the grid as a game of tic-tac-toe. Marty goes first, playing X, and Marie goes second, playing O. All of Marty's answers came out to be the same number. Who was the likely winner?

_____

3. At the end of the game, which boxes had Xs and which had Os? Mark up the completed board.

_____

$\frac{3}{4}(25 - 5) + 4(11 - 3) =$	$2(3 + 1) + 8(7 - 2) =$	$(4^2 - 3^2) + 6(3 + 4) =$
$(13 \times 2) + (8 - 1)^2 - 5^2 =$	$\frac{3}{2}(7 + 5) + 2(8 + 7) =$	$5^2 + 4(7 - 2) + 3 =$
$3^2 + 2(4^2) + \frac{1}{3}(18) =$	$3(4 \times 3) + 2(10 - 4) =$	$9^2 - 3(8 + 3) =$

Percent Problems

Solve the following percent problems.

1. On class field day, five teams competed in different events. It was possible for each team to score 60 points in all. The Zebras scored 35% of the possible 60 points. The Tigers scored 54 of the 60 possible points. The Bears scored half as many points as the Tigers. The Giraffes scored 12 fewer points than the Bears. The Lions scored $\frac{2}{5}$ of the 60 possible points. What percent of the total 60 points did each team score? List the teams' scores in descending order.

_____

_____

_____

_____

_____

2. Grace, Tristan, Maggie, Scott, and Jason each have to answer 100 questions for their geography project, but none of them is finished yet! Grace has answered $\frac{3}{5}$ of the questions. Tristan has answered 10 fewer questions than Grace. Maggie has answered half as many as Tristan. Scott has answered 0.3 of the questions. Jason has answered 6 more questions than Scott. What percent of the 100 questions has each student answered?

_____

_____

_____

_____

_____

Mental Math

Try solving each of these problems in your head. No paper and pencil allowed!

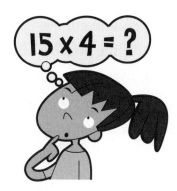

1. If a bottle of water costs $0.85, how many bottles can you buy for $10.00? _____

2. If you begin walking home at 1:35 PM and arrive at 3:01 PM, how long did it take you to get there? _____

3. If you can do 90 push-ups in 2 minutes, how many can you do in 10 minutes? _____

4. If you exercise for 40 minutes five days a week, and 55 minutes twice a week, how long have you exercised in total? _____

5. You have 8 different outfits. You wear a different one each day and do not wear it again until you've worn all the others. If you wear outfit 1 on December 1, how many times will you wear the first outfit that month? _____

6. If you play fetch with your dog for 8 minutes and then just walk with your dog for another 68 minutes, what fraction of that time was spent playing fetch? Reduce your answer to lowest terms. _____

Party Planning

Use the chart and information provided to solve the problems below.

Food	Amount
Sliced turkey	2.38 lbs
Sausage links	2.37 lbs
Potato salad	4 lbs
Egg salad	2.75 lbs
Macaroni salad	3 lbs
Hot dogs	4.4 lbs
Chicken salad	1.50 lbs
Sliced roast beef	2.8 lbs
Sliced cheese	3.02 lbs
Sliced ham	2.75 lbs

Four friends are hosting a party. They went to the store separately, and each friend bought two items from the list above. They did not get every item on the list and no two people bought the same item. Carla purchased sliced meat. Keisha bought sliced cheese and one type of sliced meat. The sliced meat Keisha purchased was the most abundant of all the sliced meats on the list. Samantha also purchased meat, but not sliced meat. The two meats Samantha got were the same shape. Allegra purchased two types of salads, one of which was potato salad. Allegra purchased one pound more of potato salad than the other salad she bought.

1. What two items and in what amount did each woman buy?

_____

_____

_____

_____

2. What items from the list did not get purchased? _____

3. The items that were not purchased each cost $1.99 per pound. You purchase both remaining items and pay with a $10.00 bill. How much change will you receive? _____

175

To Scale

Answer the following questions about scale.

1. If the Statue of Liberty's arm measures about 42 feet in length, approximately how long might her nose be? _____ How can you determine this? _____

_____

2. A model train's scale is $\frac{1}{8}$ inch = 1 foot. If the model caboose measures 4 inches long, how long is the real caboose? _____

3. Measure the dimensions of a toy car and compare them to the measurements of a real car. Does the toy appear to be a scale model of the real car? _____

4. You can enlarge pictures by using scale. Use the smaller image as a guide to help you recreate the same image, but larger, in the blank box. Simply copy what is in each cell of the smaller picture into the same cell in the blank image. Watch it grow!

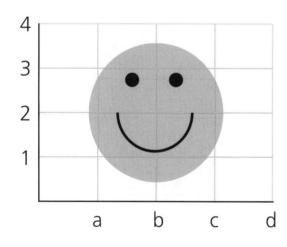

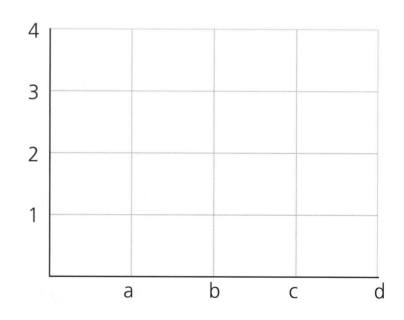

Construction Zone

Write an equation for each of the descriptions below.

1. Max moved three more bricks than twice Jim's amount.

_____

2. Tony's drill weighed four times as much as Max and Jim's combined.

_____

3. Jim collected 18 more orange cones from the site than Max collected.

_____

4. The amount of work completed by the construction team on Monday and Wednesday totaled the same amount done on Saturday and Tuesday.

_____

5. Tony carried 16 pounds less concrete mix than Max and Jim together.

_____

6. Jim laid 5 fewer bricks than Max and Tony did together.

_____

7. Max took a lunch break for five times longer than Jim did.

_____

8. On Sunday, the construction team built 7 more walls than they did on Thursday.

_____

9. To grout the tile on Monday, it took the team $\frac{1}{4}$ of the time it did to grout the tile on Tuesday.

_____

10. On Saturday, the construction team laid 3 tiles less than twice the amount laid on Monday.

_____

Good Investments

Answer the following questions about investing money.

Banker's Rule: To find the number of years needed to double an investment, divide 70 by the interest rate.

Example: Interest rate = 5%

$$70 \div 5 = 14 \text{ years}$$

1. You invest $20 at an annual interest rate of 7%. You make no withdrawals and all the interest is reinvested. How long will it take for you to double your money? _____

2. Home run champion Billy Baseball's rookie baseball card was worth $3,000 in 1927. Its value doubled every seven years. What was it worth in 2008? _____

3. With a parent or adult, go to a local bank. Find out how much annual interest you could earn on a savings account there. If you invest money at this rate, how long would it take your money to double? _____

4. You borrow $1,200 at 8% interest for 2 years. How much interest do you owe? _____

5. If you extend your loan period to 4 years, how much interest do you owe? _____
What does this tell you about loan periods? _____

_____

Right or Wrong?

You be the teacher! Determine if the answers to the problems below are correct or incorrect.
When you're finished, determine the percent that are correct and "grade" the paper.

1. $\dfrac{8}{11} = 0.727$

2. $\dfrac{15}{40} = 37.5\%$

3. $\dfrac{13}{52} = \dfrac{1}{3}$

4. $\dfrac{7}{9} \times \dfrac{4}{5} = \dfrac{28}{45}$

5. $0.429 = \dfrac{3}{7}$

6. $0.89 = 8.9\%$

7. $80\% \text{ of } 95 = 76$

8. $6\dfrac{2}{3} + 9\dfrac{4}{7} = 16\dfrac{1}{4}$

9. $4\dfrac{1}{2} \times 3\dfrac{1}{3} = 15$

10. $8\dfrac{1}{3} - 7\dfrac{5}{6} = \dfrac{1}{2}$

What is this student's grade? _____

Unlucky 13

The number 13 has many superstitions that surround it. Answer the following questions about this eerie number.

1. Use the Internet or an encyclopedia to research why the number 13 is considered by some to be unlucky. Write at least three reasons here.

_____

_____

_____

_____

_____

2. Many hotels do not have an unlucky thirteenth floor. How many floors does this hotel have altogether, including the lobby? _____

3. Study a one-dollar bill to see if you can find 13 of any one object.

_____

The Hands Have It

Do different-sized hands have different angles between the fingers? Trace your hand and the hand of a small child in the space here. Then use your protractor to measure the angles created by the fingers.

How do they compare? _____

_____

How does the length of the fingers affect this? _____

_____

Finding Congruence

Draw a line to match each polygon to its congruent polygon.

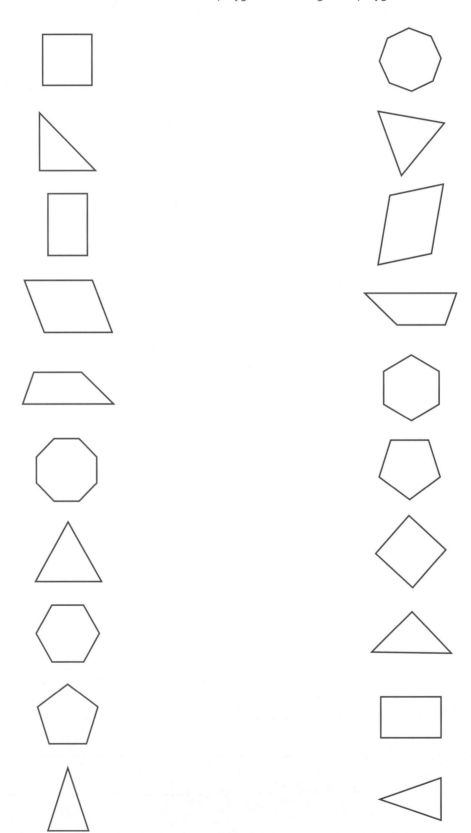

On the Road Again

Use the car flyers to solve the problems that follow.

Dellium
20 CITY/29 HIGHWAY
17.5 GALLON TANK

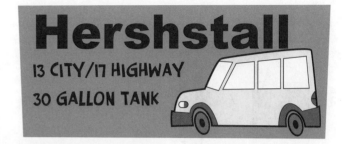

Hershstall
13 CITY/17 HIGHWAY
30 GALLON TANK

Minitroop
44 CITY/49 HIGHWAY
10.3 GALLON TANK

1. Which of these cars has the largest gas tank? _____

2. Why do you think the car from question #1 has such a large tank? _____

_____

_____

3. Which of these three cars can go the farthest on one tank of gas when driving on the highway?

_____

4. Which of these three cars can go the farthest on one tank of gas when driving in the city?

_____

5. You drive a Minitroop and commute to work five days per week. Your daily commute is 80 highway miles and 10 city miles each way. On Monday, you have a full tank of gas. When will you run out of gas? _____

Surprise Package

Use a centimeter ruler to measure each of the gift boxes below. Mark its measurements next to each side. The scale of each box is 1 cm = 10 cm. Based on this scale, determine the volume of each box. Write it on the line next to the image.

1.

_____

2.

_____

3.

_____

4.

_____

5.

_____

6.

_____

7.

_____

8.

_____

Big Dig

Use the chart to solve the problems that follow.

Site	Pottery	Ceramic Figures	Bones	Coins	Tools
A	10%	20%	0%	40%	30%
B	30%	10%	10%	0%	45%
C	0%	35%	35%	10%	20%
D	40%	0%	20%	32%	8%
E	5%	22%	30%	15%	28%

1. At five different archeological dig sites, various artifacts were found. The table shows the percentage of each type of artifact found at the sites. Which two sites seem to be the most alike and why? Show your work. _____

2. If 20 coins were collected from site C, how many tools were collected? _____

3. Which site had the largest percentage of bones and coins? _____

4. Which site had the smallest percentage of pottery and tools? _____

Answer Key

Pages 4–5
1. 10
2. 80
3. 470
4. ← 1 | 1,000 →
5. 200
6. 900
7. 4,500
8. ← 1 | 10,000 →
9. 9,000
10. 3,000
11. 23,000
12. ← 1 | 100,000 →
13. 10,000
14. 10,000
15. 20,000
16. ← 10,000 | 20,000 →
17. 300,000
18. 100,000
19. 400,000
20. ← 1 | 500,000 →

Page 6
1. 8
2. 7
3. 12
4. 4
5. 2
6. 1
7. 3
8. 3
9. 5
10. 0

Page 7
2. 8,888 + 8,521
3. 943 − 221
4. 1,047 + 39,520
5. 7,225 − 7,002
6. 64,286 − 842
7. 17 + 753
8. 63 + 2,367
9. 289,002 − 2,756
10. 826 + 7,321

Page 8
1. hundred thousands
2. ten millions
3. $7,625,000.00
4. ten thousands
5. hundreds; $14,375,500.00
6. millions
7. thousands; twenty-four thousand dollars
8. $3,500,000.00

Page 9
1. 13,431
2. 1,551
3. 1,221

Page 10
1. $\frac{1}{2}$
2. $\frac{1}{4}$
3. $\frac{1}{7}$
4. $\frac{1}{5}$
5. $\frac{2}{3}$
6. $\frac{1}{10}$
7. $\frac{4}{5}$

8. Marsha
9. Steve
10. Tom

Page 11

Page 12
1. 1,667 feet
2. 1,483 feet
3. One thousand, four hundred fifty-one feet
4. One thousand, three hundred sixty-two feet
5. 2,627,138
6. 1,297,526
7. Shanghai
8. 13,000,000

Page 13
Answers will vary.

Page 14
1.
```
    72
11)792
    77
    22
```
Line should connect to chocolate chips.

2.
```
    40
22)880
   88
   00
```
Line should connect to chocolate sauce bottle.

3.
```
    3
31)93
   93
    0
```
Line should connect to whipped cream.

4.
```
     87
15)1,305
   120
   105
   105
     0
```
Line should connect to caramel sauce.

5.
```
     58
79)4,582
   395
   632
   632
     0
```
Line should connect to cherries.

Page 15
1. $11.70
2. corduroy pants
3. peacoats
4. $65.99
5. $29.75

6. wool socks
7. cashmere sweaters
8. cotton hoodies
9. $33.99
10. peacoats

Pages 16–17
1.
2. 29
3. −29
4.
5. 8
6. 8
7. 9 degrees
8. 10 degrees
9. High of −3°F, Low of −16°F
10. High of 16°F, Low of 11°F
11.
12. 13
13.
14. 4

Page 18
1. $\frac{1}{6}$
2. $\frac{1}{4}$
3. $\frac{5}{12}$
4. $\frac{1}{12}$
5. $\frac{1}{12}$
6. 10:5
7. 25:60
8. 15:5
9. red; 25 > 5
10. orange; 5 < 15

Page 19
1. 0.016; 0.1; 0.13; 0.136; 1.36
2. 0.03; 0.123; 0.132; 0.30; 1.23
3. 0.08; 0.12; 0.51; 0.6; 0.65
4. 4.02; 4.0; 3.56; 3.546; 3.49
5. 106.25; 101.04; 101.0; 100.9; 10.10
6. 1.95; 1.88; 1.80; 1.59; 1.31
7. 3.116
8. 0.13

Page 20
1. COMPLETE
2.
```
      42
     /  \
    7    6
        / \
       2   3
```
3. COMPLETE
4.
```
       24
      /  \
     4    6
    / \  / \
   2  2 2   3
```
5.
```
      30
     /  \
    5    6
        / \
       2   3
```
6.
```
      56
     /  \
    7    8
        / \
       4   2
      / \
     2   2
```
7.
```
      63
     /  \
    9    7
   / \
  3   3
```
8. COMPLETE
9.
```
       90
      /  \
     9    10
    / \   / \
   3  3  2   5
```

Page 21
1. Ben $\frac{23}{8}$ → $2\frac{3}{4}$
2. Jennifer $\frac{27}{8}$ → $1\frac{4}{5}$
3. Margaret $\frac{25}{6}$ → $2\frac{7}{8}$
4. Courtney $\frac{11}{4}$ → $3\frac{3}{8}$
5. Jesse $\frac{9}{5}$ → $4\frac{1}{6}$
6. $\frac{31}{8}$
7. $\frac{21}{5}$
8. $\frac{31}{10}$
9. Jake; Jesse
10. $\frac{12}{5} = 2\frac{2}{5}$

Pages 22–23
1. poodle
   Labrador retriever
   shih tzu
   golden retriever
   rottweiler
   terrier
   dalmation
   foxhound
   pug
2. 4
3. 0
4. 3
5. 5
6. <

7. >
8. >
9. <
10. >
11. −6
12. 8
13. −3
14. 7
15. 27
16. −17
17. 2
18. 0
19. −20
20. −16

Page 24
1.
	7		
4.7		2.3	
4.19	0.51		1.79
4	0.19	0.32	1.47
3.98	0.02	0.17	0.15	1.32

2.
	42.1		
22		20.1	
10.3	11.7		8.4
4.3	6.0	5.7	2.7
1.7	2.6	3.4	2.3	0.4

3.
	8.22		
4.24		3.98	
2.1	2.14		1.84
0.96	1.14	1	0.84
0.2	0.76	0.38	0.62	0.22

4.
	10.57		
5.75		4.82	
2.53	3.22		1.6
0.77	1.76	1.46	0.14
0.37	0.4	1.36	0.1	0.04

5.
	14.728		
7.82		6.908	
4.626	3.194		3.714
2.706	1.92	1.274	2.44
1.92	0.786	1.134	0.14	2.3

6.
	8.814		
3.384		5.43	
1.324	2.06		3.37
0.564	0.76	1.3	2.07
0.004	0.56	0.2	1.1	0.97

Page 25
1. Baseball All Stars 2009
   Rock Star 2009 Edition
   Military Man
   Pop Band
   Superbug!
   Baseball All Stars 2008
   Total Enforcement
2. Three Pop Bands; $51.00
3. One Military Man; $38.01
4. Superbug!; Baseball All Stars 2008; Total Enforcement
5. $10; 20%

Page 26
1. 1:30
2. 8:45
3. 12:15
4. The second clock at 8:45 PM
5. The third clock at 12:15 AM
6.
7.
8.

Page 27
1. Answers will vary but must include five points from A through U.
2. $\overline{KO}$ and $\overline{NL}$
3. Answers will vary but must include: $\overrightarrow{BA}$, $\overline{CD}$, $\overline{MK}$, $\overrightarrow{MO}$, $\overline{ML}$, $\overline{MN}$.
4. Answers will vary, but must include: AB, BC, CD, EF, FG, EG, FI, HI, IJ, HJ, KM, KO, MO, NL, NM, ML, PS, QT, RU, PQ, QR, PR.
5. Answers will vary but include: AB and CD; EF and HI; FG and IJ; EG and HJ; PS and QT; QT and RU; PS and RU.
6. Answers will vary but must include: F, I, M, N, W, Z.
7. Answers will vary but must include: EF and FI; GF and FI; JI and IF; HI and IF; KM and ML; LM and MO; MO and MN; MN and MK; PS and PQ; QR and RU; PQ and QT; QT and QR; EG and FI; HJ and FI; KO and LN; KO and ML; KO and MN; LN and KM; LN and MO; PR and QT.
8. Answers will vary, but must include F, I, L, T.

Page 28
1. C
2. N
3. P
4. A
5. K
6. C
7. N
8. Q
9. G
10. O

Page 29
1. 393 feet
2. 240 feet
3. 500 yards
4. 28.26 meters
5. 200 meters

Pages 30–31
1. Russia
   Ukraine
   Latvia
   Germany
   Slovakia
   Czech Republic
2. United States
   Hungary
   Germany
   France
3. Germany
   Ukraine
   Great Britain
   Kenya
   France
4. Poland
5. United States
6. Germany
7. United States
8. Germany
9. 2,624 feet; 328 feet; 1,312 feet
10. 5.39

Page 32
Answers will vary.

Page 33
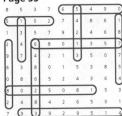

Pages 34–35
1. False
2. True
3. True
4. False
5. False
6. Cedar Center Plaza
7. La Place & Beachwood Malls
8. Answers will vary, but two possible routes are:
   Go north on North Park Blvd. Turn right at Cedar Road and follow it to the intersection of Richmond Road.
   Go east on Fairmont Blvd. and turn left at Richmond Road. Follow it until it intersects with Cedar Road.

Page 36
1. 90°F

168

2. 30°F

83

3. −20° F

36

Page 37
1. $\frac{3}{4}$; 0.75
2. $\frac{1}{2}$; 0.5
3. Himalayas Parka; $39.50
4. Alps Parka and Himalayas Parka
5. Alps Parka
6. $\frac{6}{18} = \frac{1}{3}$

Page 38
1. −4, 4, 8, 18, 20
2. −32, −30, 3, 30, 32
3. −3, −1, 0, 1, 10
4. −6, 0, 5, 6, 9
5. >; 4
6. >; 6
7. <; 5
8. >; 3

Page 39
1. acute; 25
2. acute; 45
3. right; 90
4. obtuse; 110
5. obtuse; 135

Page 40
Answers will vary, but must include:
1.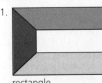
rectangle
2.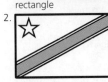
triangle, trapezoid, or star.
3.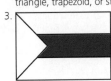
triangle or trapezoid.

Page 41
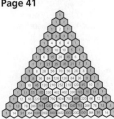
1. triangles
2. four
3. five, including the large triangle that encompasses the others

Page 42
1. 1,932 square inches; 81" × 40"; 242 inches
2. 576 square inches; 34" × 34"; 136 inches
3. 2,736 square inches; 86" × 52"; 276 inches

Page 43
1. $2 \times 2 \times 5 \times 3$ or $2^2 \times 5 \times 3$
2. $5 \times 3 \times 3$ or 5×3^2
3. $5 \times 2 \times 2$ or 5×2^2
4. $11 \times 2 \times 3$
5. 5×5 or 5^2
6. $2 \times 2 \times 2 \times 2 \times 2 \times 2$ or 2^6
7. $2 \times 2 \times 2 \times 2 \times 2$ or 2^5
8. $3 \times 2 \times 2 \times 2$ or 3×2^3
9. $3 \times 3 \times 3 \times 3$ or 3^4
10. 5×2
11. $2 \times 2 \times 2 \times 2 \times 2 \times 3$ or 3×2^5
12. $2 \times 2 \times 3 \times 7$ or $2^2 \times 3 \times 7$

Page 44
1. 26
2. 15
3. 20
4. −1
5. 6
6. 8
7. 89
8. 39
9. 10
10. 28
MATH RULES!

Page 41 (right column)
4.
hexagon or triangle.
5.
star or circle.
6.
rectangle or square.

Page 45
1. the number of hours Sam watched television; the number of hours Sam's competitor watched television
2. dates of the Emmy Awards; the number of Emmy Awards won in 2009 or after
3. the national average
4. the height of the cabinet
5. the rankings of the other shows for that week
6. the sale price of, or discount on, the 42-inch television

Page 46

Page 47
1. c and a; 16 cats
2. c; 60% are mixed breeds
3. a, b, and c; 5,000 square feet
4. a and c; 5 weeks
5. a and b; 29 ½ hours

Pages 48–49
1. 10 tablespoons butter
   6 tablespoons flour
   5 cups milk
   2 lbs cheddar cheese
   1 lb Colby cheese
   2 tablespoons Dijon mustard
   $\frac{1}{4}$ teaspoon nutmeg
   $\frac{1}{4}$ teaspoon cayenne pepper
   $\frac{1}{2}$ teaspoon each salt and pepper
   2 lbs elbow macaroni
   $1\frac{1}{2}$ cups bread crumbs
2. $2\frac{1}{2}$ tablespoons butter
   $1\frac{1}{2}$ tablespoons flour
   $1\frac{1}{4}$ cups milk
   $\frac{1}{2}$ lb cheddar cheese
   $\frac{1}{4}$ lb Colby cheese
   $\frac{1}{2}$ tablespoon Dijon mustard
   $\frac{1}{16}$ teaspoon nutmeg
   $\frac{1}{16}$ teaspoon cayenne pepper
   $\frac{1}{8}$ teaspoon each salt and pepper
   $\frac{1}{2}$ lb elbow macaroni
   about $\frac{1}{3}$ cup breadcrumbs
3. $\frac{1}{2}$ onion
   $\frac{3}{4}$ clove garlic
   $\frac{1}{4}$ lb lean ground beef
   $\frac{1}{2}$ cup diced tomatoes
   $\frac{3}{8}$ cup tomato paste
   $\frac{1}{4}$ cup beef broth

$\frac{1}{4}$ tablespoon cumin

$\frac{1}{4}$ teaspoon oregano

$\frac{1}{4}$ teaspoon coriander

$\frac{1}{4}$ teaspoon salt

$1\frac{3}{4}$ ounces black beans

1 chili pepper

4. 6 onions

9 cloves garlic

3 lbs lean ground beef

6 cups diced tomatoes

$4\frac{1}{2}$ cups tomato paste

3 cups beef broth

3 tablespoons cumin

3 teaspoons oregano

3 teaspoons coriander

3 teaspoons salt

21 ounces black beans

12 chili peppers

Page 50
1. $0.55
2. $1.34
3. $0.12
4. $1.01
5. $1.69
6. $0.20 per pound
7. 2 pounds
8. 5 pounds
9. 2.8 pounds
10. 3 pounds

Page 51
1. 900,000
2. 100,000
3. 600,000
4. 100,353
5. 1,000,000
6. 4,000,000
7. 8,000,000
8. 8,250,823
9. 3,000,000,000
10. 1,000,000,000
11. 7,000,000,000
12. 6,707,590,132

Page 52
1. years
2. number of lunches purchased
3. 2006
4. 2004
5. b
6. d

Page 53
1. $\frac{1}{3}$ hour

20 minutes

2. $\frac{1}{2}$ hour

30 minutes

3. $1\frac{5}{6}$ hour

110 minutes

4. $\frac{11}{12}$ hour

55 minutes

5. $\frac{1}{2}$ hour

30 minutes

Page 54
1. The following should be underlined: where he spent four nights at a hotel that cost $199.00 per night; to all the tourist desinations

599 miles

2. The following should be underlined: The uniforms cost $75.00 each, plus tax.

312

3. The following should be underlined: The winner was a surprising 58 year old, while the average age of all the runners was only 32.

419

4. The following should be underlined: Even though Jane lives in New York City and walks about 4 miles per day, she still wears high-heeled shoes all the time.

$1,800.00

5. The following should be underlined: After work today, 6 of which were anchovy, 4 of which were plain cheese, and 2 of which had mushrooms and peppers.

4 slices

Page 55
1. $\frac{1}{2} + \frac{3}{4}$
2. $\frac{3}{5} + \frac{1}{10}$
3. $\frac{1}{2} + \frac{1}{3}$
4. $\frac{1}{3} + \frac{1}{5}$
5. $\frac{2}{3} - \frac{1}{5}$
6. $\frac{7}{8} - \frac{3}{8}$
7. $\frac{3}{4} - \frac{1}{3}$
8. $\frac{1}{2} - \frac{1}{6}$

Page 56
1. The following should be shaded: 2, 4, 6, 8, 10, 20, 28, 56, 70
2. The following should be circled: 3, 6, 15, 21
3. The following should be shaded: 1, 2, 3, 5, 7
4. The following should be circled: 4, 6, 8, 10, 15, 20, 21, 28, 35, 56, 70
5. The following should be shaded: 7, 21, 28, 35, 56, 70
6. The following should be circled: 10, 20, 70
7. The following should be shaded: 4, 8, 20, 28, 56
8. The following should be circled: 5, 10, 15, 20, 35, 70

Page 57
1. b
2. a
3. c
4. c
5. a
6. b
7. a
8. c

Page 58
1. true
2. false; Numbers that are subtracted are not commutative.
3. true
4. true
5. false; Numbers that are divided are not commutative.
6. true
7. false; Numbers that are divided are not commutative.
8. true
9. true
10. true

Page 59
1. 02/08 to 03/08
2. 6,600,400,000
   6,606,900,000
   6,613,500,000
   6,619,800,000
   6,626,400,000
   6,632,700,000
   6,639,200,000
   6,645,800,000
   6,651,900,000
   6,658,400,000
   6,664,700,000
   6,671,300,000
   6,677,600,000
3. six billion, six hundred million, four hundred eleven thousand, fifty-one; six billion, six hundred six million, nine hundred forty-nine thousand, one hundred six; six billion, six hundred thirteen million, four hundred eighty-four thousand, one hundred sixty-two

Page 60
1. 99.6 mph; swinging strike
2. 97.9 mph; foul
3. 2:3
4. 3:7
5. 98.7
6. 98.7

Page 61
1. about 14 inches
2. about 35 or 36 centimeters
3. about 2.54
4. 1 foot, two inches or 1' 2"

Page 62
1. 6 squares
2. 2 triangles, 3 rectangles
3. 4 rectangles, 2 squares
4. 5 rectangles, 2 squares, 2 triangles
5. 4 triangles, 1 square
6. 2 squares, 4 rectangles

Page 63
1. 53 + 15 + 3;
   15 + 3 + 53; 71 marbles
2. 6 × 8; 8 × 6; 48 oranges
3. 42 × 6 × 75; 6 × 75 × 42; 18,900 books
4. 3 + 6 + 2; 6 + 2 + 3; 11 treats
5. 3 × 1; 1 × 3; 3 quarts of trash

Pages 64–65
1. Thursday
2. Tuesday
3. Friday
4. Thursday; It's going to be sunny, warm, and clear, with no rain.
5. Monday
6. 10%; $\frac{1}{10}$
7. 70%; $\frac{7}{10}$
8. 86°F
9. 67°F
10. Wednesday because it's going to be the breeziest, but it probably won't rain.
11. About 40.5°F
12. About 48.8°F
13. 56°F
14. About 51.2°F
15. About 58.6°F

Page 66

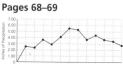

1. 1,234,567
2. 2,345,678
3. 98,765,432
4. 980,421
5. 76,543,210

Page 67
1. eight
2. three
3. ten
4. five
5. four
6. six
7. seven
8. four
9. three
10. eight

Pages 68–69

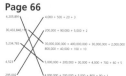

1. 44.64 inches
2. June was the wettest and February was the driest.
3. 3.72 inches
4. 3.88
5. 3.81

Page 70
1. true
2. true
3. false; Numbers that are subtracted are not associative.
4. true
5. false; Numbers that are divided are not associative.
6. true
7. true
8. false; Numbers that are divided are not associative.
9. true
10. false; Numbers that are subtracted are not associative.

Page 71
1. 16
2. 9
3. 24
4. 64
5. $\frac{1}{2}$ cup
6. $16\frac{2}{3}$
7. 18
8. $2\frac{1}{4}$

Pages 72–73
Answers will vary.

Page 74

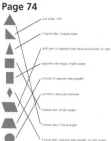

one angle = 90°

2 equal sides, 2 equal angles

both pairs of opposite sides equal and parallel, no right angles

opposite sides equal, 4 right angles

one pair of opposite sides parallel

symmetric about any diameter

4 equal sides, 4 right angles

3 equal sides, 3 equal angles

4 equal sides, opposite sides parallel, no right angles

Page 75
1. C
2. AB and DE
3. radii
4. ACF or DCF
5. chord
6. segment
7. 4 inches
8. 8 inches
9. 90°
10. 25°

Page 76
1. $\frac{2}{8}$ or $\frac{1}{4}$
2. $\frac{5}{8}$
3. $\frac{1}{8}$
4. $\frac{7}{8}$
5. $\frac{6}{8}$ or $\frac{3}{4}$
6. B
7. C
8. A
9. A
10. C

Page 77
1. 2
2. 2
3. 3
4. 3*a* and 2*t*
5. 2*n*, *n*, and 7*k*
6. 3*p*
7. L
8. U
9. U
10. 9
11. $\frac{1}{2}$
12. 7

Pages 78–79
1. 56.2
2. 5.73
3. 2.86
4. 23.87
5. 8.224
6. 45.69
7. 0.2
8. 123.555

Page 80
1. <; 3 quarts = 0.75 gallon OR 36 quarts = 9 gallons
2. =
3. =
4. >; 3 pounds = 48 ounces OR 2.06 pounds = 33 ounces
5. =
6. =
7. >; 2 yards = 72 inches OR 1.67 yards = 60 inches
8. >; 5 gallons = 20 quarts OR 4.5 gallons = 18 quarts
9. =
10. >; 5 pints = 2.5 quarts OR 4 pints = 2 quarts

Page 81
1. multiply; $284.00
2. multiply and add; $157.00
3. multiply; yes
4. divide; 4
5. multiply and add; Seven Flags season passes for everyone
6. divide; 4
7. add and subtract; $33.00
8. multiply and add; yes

Page 82
1. b
2. a
3. c
4. b
5. Erik
6. home or 0
7. Danielle
8. This question is correct if (−2,0) is marked and labeled "Charlotte."

Page 83
Answers will vary.

Page 84

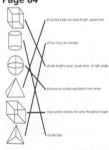

Page 85
1. incorrect; $\frac{f}{10} = 1.62$
2. incorrect; $0.2c − b = −2.06$
3. correct
4. correct
5. incorrect; $d + e − c = f + 7.7$
6. correct
7. correct
8. 6.4 miles away
9. 5.4 miles
10. 170.4 miles

Page 86
1. $4a + 4b$
2. $14c − 21d + 35$

3. $7 \times 8 = 56$
4. $2(a + b)$
5. $ab + 4a − 3b − 12$
6. $5 \times 5 = 25$
7. $xz + 2x − 5z − 10$
8. $14a + 21b$
9. $6c − 6d + 12$
10. $5(2c − 4d + 6)$

Page 87
1. Martin
2. Mrs. Lindgren and Jackie
3. 6 PM
4. 3 PM
5. Martin, James, and Grandma
6. Martin and Grandma
7. 3 hours
8. Grandma

Page 88
1. 0; additive
2. 2; additive
3. 1; multiplicative
4. 3; multiplicative
5. 0; additive
6. 11; multiplicative
7. 12; additive
8. 12; multiplicative
9. 0; additive
10. 1; multiplicative

Page 89
1. d
2. a
3. b
4. c
5. c
6. b
7. Answers will vary.
8. Answers will vary.

Page 90
1. a
2. b
3. d
4. a
5. c

Page 91
1. add 7, subtract 4
2. subtract 4, add 3
3. add 5
4. subtract 3, add 10
5. add 3, subtract 1
6. Answers will vary.
7. Answers will vary.
8. Answers will vary.
9. Answers will vary.
10. Answers will vary.

Pages 92–93
1. $17.75
2. $14.90; $0.75
3. $21.75; $1.74
4. $48.85; $46.41
5. $14.00; $12.60
6. $36.50; $31.02; $1.55
7. $34.20; $30.78; $2.15; $6.16
8. $276.25; $221.00; $12.16; $33.15; $266.31

Pages 94–95
Answers to questions 1–5 will vary, but may include the following numbers:
1. 15, 30, 45, 60, 75
2. 21, 42, 63, 84, 105
3. 30, 60, 90, 120, 150
4. 16, 32, 48, 64, 80

5. 20, 40, 60, 80, 100
6. 60
7. 30
8. 60
9. 252
10. 750
11. yes
12. 24
13. 60 pounds
14. 42 to 42
15. 24 to 24

Page 96

Page 97
1. food; pet care
2. $200.00
3. $300.00
4. $66.67
5. $233.33
6. pet care; it would probably double to $\frac{1}{6}$ or $133.33
7. $\frac{3}{24} = \frac{1}{8}$
8. $\frac{1}{10}$

Page 98
1. 1,000 cubic units
2. 1,500 cubic units
3. 113.04 cubic centimeters
4. 20.93 cubic centimeters
5. 480 cubic units
6. 1,099 cubic centimeters
7. 2,143.57 cubic centimeters
8. 147 cubic centimeters

Page 99
1. 15
2. 20
3. 5
4. 23
5. 8
6. 20
7.

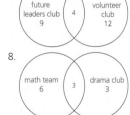

8.

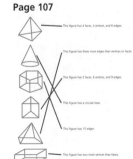

Page 100
1. a
2. b
3. b
4. c

Page 101
1. Baxter
2. 6
3. Baxter
4. Baxter
5. no
6. Lady
7. Baxter
8. 2002

Page 102
1. similar
2. congruent
3. congruent
4. similar
5. neither
6. congruent
7. neither
8. similar
9. congruent
10. congruent

Page 103
1. May
2. January
3. August
4. August
5. March
6. 48°F
7. $26\frac{1}{2}$°F
8. There are two modes: 26 and 49

Page 104
1. 5
2. 6
3. 2
4. 4
5. 1
6. 4 paper bills, 8 coins
7. 2 quarters and 2 pennies; 52 pennies
8. $0.99; 9 coins: 3 quarters, 2 dimes, 4 pennies

Page 105
1. 19°C
2. −4°C
3. 34°C
4. 13°C
5. −11°C
6. °F = $\frac{9}{5}$°C + 32
7. 81°F
8. 3°F
9. 104°F
10. 25°F

Page 106
1. 1 PM
2. Saturday
3. Amber
4. Betsy
5. 17
6. squash

Page 107

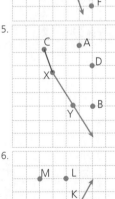

Page 108

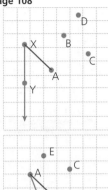

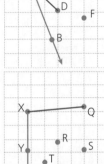

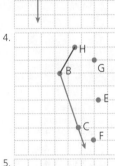

Page 109
Answers will vary.

Page 110
1. 75.36 inches
2. 8.60 inches
3. 62.80 inches
4. 5.34 inches
5. 21.98 feet
6. 6.37 meters

Page 111
1. $500.00; 5%; 2 years
2. $2,625.00
3. $7,200.00
4. 5%
5. $7,500.00
6. 30 years
7. $2,000.00; $6,000
8. $88.00; $888.00

Pages 112–113

Employee	Time In	Time Out	Number of Hours Worked	Hourly Wage	Total Wage Earned
Nina	7:00 AM	5:00 PM	10	$7.50	$75.00
Jerry	6:50 AM	4:20 PM	9½	$6.95	$66.03
Neo	7:07 AM	4:07 PM	9	$8.00	$72.00
Cheyenne	7:45 AM	5:45 PM	10	$7.50	$75.00
Scott	8:30 AM	4:30 PM	8	$8.25	$66.00
Elan	8:01 AM	6:31 PM	10½	$9.50	$99.75
Waldorf	7:35 AM	4:35 PM	9	$9.00	$81.00
Dashon	8:10 AM	4:40 PM	8½	$7.75	$65.88
Oscar	7:55 AM	4:55 PM	9	$8.00	$72.00
Harper	7:20 AM	3:50 PM	8½	$6.95	$59.08
Lee	7:57 AM	5:57 PM	10	$9.25	$92.50

1. Elan
2. Scott
3. Elan
4. Jerry
5. Harper
6. There are three modes: $6.95, $7.50, and $8.00.
7. $8.06
8. $62.55
9. $85.50
10. $4.00

Page 114
1. b
2. a
3. d
4. b
5. d
6. a
7. 4 ounces
8. 1.62 ounces
9. 3,000 pounds
10. 5 pounds

Page 115
1. b
2. b
3. a
4. d
5. c
6. c

Page 116
1. 30
2. 10
3. 28
4. 13.5
5. 31.5
6. 80
7. 4.5
8. 36
9. 96
10. 59.5
11. 44

GEOMETRY FUN!

Page 117
1. 87
2. 18 flowers, 14 seashells
3. no; $24.47
4. 24 red balloons
   20 purple balloons
   12 green balloons
   24 yellow balloons
   12 orange hats
   27 blue hats
   6 white hats
   15 pink hats

Pages 118–119
1.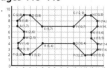

2. a bone
3.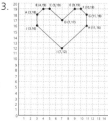

4. a heart

Page 120
2.29 cups flour
1 teaspoon baking soda
1 teaspoon salt
1.04 cups butter
0.73 cup granulated sugar
0.73 cup brown sugar
1 teaspoon vanilla extract
2 eggs
Two 5.88 oz. packages
   chocolate chips
1.04 cups chopped nuts

Preheat the oven to 374°F. In small bowl, combine flour, baking soda, and salt; set aside. In large bowl, combine butter, sugar, brown sugar, and vanilla; beat until creamy. Beat in eggs. Gradually add flour mixture; mix well. Stir in chocolate chips and nuts. Bake 8 to 10 minutes.

Page 121
1. 5
2. 7
3. Shoes
4. 3
5. true
6. Ground Level Cafe
7. 6
8. Men's Clothing

Pages 122–123
1. 11
2. 26
3. 9
4. 40
5. 167
6. 59
7. 43
8. 16
9. 99
10. 49
11. 267
12. 717
13. 3,281
14. Answers will vary.
15. Answers will vary.
16. Answers will vary.

Page 124
1. Allison's address is 526 Altamont Hill. Craig's address is 562 Altamont Hill. Jessica's address is 263 Altamont Hill. Keith's address is 362 Altamont Hill. Larry's address is 265 Altamont Hill. Renee's address is 262 Altamont Hill.
2. Jessica's house is brown. Larry's house is red. Renee's house is yellow. 260 Altamont Hill is the orange house. 267 Altamont Hill is the purple house. 261 Altamont Hill is the blue house.

Page 125
1. Parentheses, Exponents, Multiplication, Division, Addition, Subtraction
2. A
3. 219 letters
4. Mercury, Venus, Earth, Mars, Jupiter, Saturn, Uranus, Neptune,
5. 5
6. 44

Page 126
1. obtuse
2. right
3. acute
4. right
5. obtuse
6. right
7. acute
8. obtuse
9. acute
10. right

Page 127
1. Left: 23 oz.
   Right: 28 oz.
2. Left: 14 oz.
   Right: 35 oz.
3. Left: 14 and 19 oz.
   Right: 23 oz.
4. Left: 23 and 35 oz.
   Right: 14 oz.
5. Left: 35 oz.
   Right: 23 and 28 oz.
6. Left: 14, 19 and 23 oz.
   Right: 28 and 35 oz.

Page 128
1. 9
2.

Student 1	Student 2	Outcome
Rock	Rock	tie
	Paper	2 wins
	Scissors	1 wins
Paper	Rock	1 wins
	Paper	tie
	Scissors	2 wins
Scissors	Rock	2 wins
	Paper	1 wins
	Scissors	tie

3. $\frac{3}{9}$ or $\frac{1}{3}$
4. $\frac{3}{9}$ or $\frac{1}{3}$

5. Yes, because both players have an equal chance of winning, losing, or tying.
6. student 1

Page 129
1. 6

chicken   beef   cheese
circle rectangle circle rectangle circle rectangle

2. 50%
3. $\frac{1}{6}$
4. 9

bone   hydrant   newspaper
red blue yellow red blue yellow red blue yellow
5. 60
6. 27
bone   hydrant   newspaper
red blue yellow red blue yellow red blue yellow
s pb gs pb gs pb gs pb gs pb gs pb gs pb gs pb g

7. $\frac{9}{27} = \frac{1}{3}$
8. $\frac{3}{27} = \frac{1}{9}$

Page 130

	Stacy	Maya	Jason	Jack
Frame 1	6	8	8	28
Frame 2	9	17	20	20
Frame 3	20	7	18	20
Frame 4	18	16	8	19
Frame 5	9	8	8	9
Frame 6	17	10	20	9
Frame 7	7	0	20	30
Frame 8	9	9	28	22
Frame 9	18	9	19	20
Frame 10	8	9	9	10
Total	121	93	158	187

1. Jack
2. 23 points
3. Maya

Page 131

sum — Substitute given values for the variables and perform the operations to find the value of the expression.
expression — The result of subtraction.
evaluate — A number, variable, or combination of numbers, variables, and operation signs.
difference — The sum of any number and 0 is that number.
variable — The answer to an addition problem.
identity property of addition — A letter or symbol that represents a number in an algebraic expression.

Page 132
1. Matthew
2. David
3. Martha
4. Matthew and David
5. Martha and Danielle
6. They are cousins.

Page 133
1. $1.78
2. 2:51
3. 2
4. 5
5. 3

Page 134
1. 168
2. 86,400
3. 10,080
4. 8,784
5. 1,200
6. 520
7. 525,600
8. 365,250
9. 1,040
10. 44,640

Page 135
Garden 1: Brian; perimeter = 32 ft, area = 48 ft²
Garden 2: Stewart; perimeter = 26 ft, area = 40 ft²
Garden 3: Jonah; perimeter = 28 ft, area = 48 ft²
Garden 4: Rosa; perimeter = 30 ft, area = 32 ft²

Page 136
1. Pacific Standard Time
2. Alaskan Standard Time
3. Answers will vary but should be one of the following: Maine, Vermont, New Hampshire, Massachusetts, New York, Rhode Island, Connecticut, New Jersey, Pennsylvania, Ohio, Michigan, Indiana, Kentucky, West Virginia, Virginia, Maryland, Washington D.C., Delaware, North Carolina, South Carolina, Tennessee, Georgia, or Florida.
4. Answers will vary but should be one of the following: Montana, Idaho, Wyoming, Utah, Colorado, New Mexico, Arizona, Nebraska, South Dakota, North Dakota, Kansas, or Texas.
5. 4 PM
6. 8 AM

Page 137
Answers will vary.

Page 138

Store
Quigley (0, 5)   Higgins (2, 5)
Willis (3, 4)
Costner (1, 4)   Restaurant
Smith (1, 1)   Bright (5, 1)
Street Entrance

Page 139
1. a
2. b
3. b
4. c
5. b
6. a

Page 140
1. c
2. a
3. b
4. c
5. b
6. b

Page 141

Page 142

1.
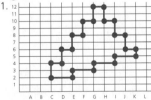

2. 175 meters
3. 150 meters
4. 100 meters
5. 300 meters
6. 11 centimeters

Page 143

Answers will vary.

Pages 144-145

1. 33 car banners
   27 sports bottles
   15 hats
   12 T-shirts
2. There will be two 8-year-olds, two 10-year-olds, and four 11-year-olds.
3. January 2: −5°F
   January 9: −1°F
   January 16: 1°F
   January 23: −2°F
   January 30: 5°F

Pages 146–147

1. Chocolate
   Vanilla
   Pistachio
   Mint Chip
   Strawberry
2. Mary
3. Meat lasagna
4. Boden Whitman

Page 148

1. A circular manhole cover will not fall through the hole because its width is the same all around. A rectangular manhole cover wouldn't work because the cover could fall through the hole when tipped upward.
2. No, neither shape would be a good manhole cover because their widths are not the same all the way around.
3. No, triangles will also fall through a hole when tipped upward—even equilateral triangles.

Page 149

1. Answers will vary.
2. b
3. b
4. a
5. b
6. parallel; 180 degrees

Page 150

1. Adam lives in Seattle, Washington.
   Marsha lives in East Blue Hill, Maine.
   George lives in San Francisco, California.
   Donna lives in Austin, Texas.
   Edward lives in Chicago, Illinois.
   Rachel lives in Fort Lauderdale, Florida
2. 3.11; 2.59
3. Fort Lauderdale; Austin
4. East Blue Hill; The precipitation amounts are consistent throughout the year.

Page 151

1.

PUMPKIN   APPLE   KEY LIME   PEACH

2. Avery chose key lime pie.
   Dillon chose pumpkin pie.
   Liam chose peach pie.
   Sierra chose apple pie.

3. Avery ate $\frac{1}{12}$
   Dillon ate $\frac{1}{8}$
   Liam ate $\frac{1}{8}$
   Sierra ate $\frac{2}{15}$

Page 152

1. 17 square feet
2. 1.35 square yards
3. 3.08 square meters
4. 12 square meters
5. 90 square meters
6. 43.4 square meters
7. 60 square yards
8. 24 square feet

Page 153

1. Yes; four 33-cent stamps and three 15-cent stamps.
2. Yes; either nine 33-cent stamps and twelve 15-cent stamps OR twenty-three 15-cent stamps and four 33-cent stamps;
3. Yes; thirty-two 33-cent stamps and forty-eight 15-cent stamps OR one hundred and three 15-cent stamps and seven 33-cent stamps.
4. 11.1%

Page 154

1.

2. The corner of 12th and H Streets OR (H,12)
3. 6:15 PM

Page 155

1. 64,000
2. 59,280
3. 27
4. They ran out of phone number combinations using the original area code.

Pages 156–157

1. $57.00; $3.99; $11.40; $72.39
2. $48.00; $3.36; $9.60; $60.96
3. $165.00; $11.55; $33.00; $209.55
4. $80.00; $5.60; $16.00; $101.60
5. $112; $7.84; $22.40; $142.24
6. $158; $11.06; $31.60; $200.66
7. $67; $4.69; $13.40; $85.09
8. $147; $10.29; $29.40; $186.69

Page 158

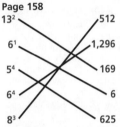

1. 1,000,000
2. 1,600
3. 2,916
4. 1,080,000
5. 1,440
6. 43,200

Page 159

1. The volume of the shorter cylinder is about 82 cubic inches, and the volume of the taller cylinder is about 63 cubic inches.
2. Any size square, as long as each is the same size.
3. Maybe: if they are bent into rectangles that have identical dimensions.
4. Answers will vary.

Page 160

1. inches
2. seconds
3. feet
4. feet
5. miles
6. ounces
7. feet
8. minutes
9. ounces
10. inches

Page 161

1. 90
2. 30
3. 22
4. 8
5. 29
6. 31
7. 9
8. 12
9. 632
10. 774
CONTINENTAL DIVIDE
Definition: The watershed of North America comprising the line of highest points of land separating the waters flowing W from those flowing N or E, coinciding with various ranges of the Rockies, and extending SSE from NW Canada to NW South America

Page 162

1. A and E
2. C and E
3. Answers will vary.
4. Answers will vary.
5. Answers will vary.

Page 163

1.
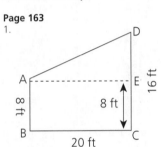

2. 22 boxes

Page 164

1. $t = 8$
2. $x = 13$
3. $n = 1$
4. $q = 5$
5. $b = 176$
6. $p = 6$
7. $g = 17$
8. $y = 12$
9. $x = 11$
10. These numbers are circled: 34, 25, 43, 80 circled.

Page 165

1. You would have to estimate how long it might take each person to buy a ticket. If each person takes 30 seconds to buy a ticket, then the 299 people in front of you will take about $2\frac{1}{2}$ hours.
2. About 600 feet away; estimate that each person takes up about 2 feet of line space. 299 people would fill about 598 feet of space, so you'd be standing 600 feet away.
3. About 10; estimate that it would take 30 seconds for each person to buy a ticket. At that rate, there would have to be 10 ticket windows open to sell 600 tickets in 30 minutes.
4. Answers will vary.

Page 166
1. $0.75
2. $118.75
3. Gabe, Josh, Andy, Wendy, Baron
4. three quarters, six dimes, and two pennies
5. One order of onion rings, OR one milk, OR one order of french fries, OR one soda, OR one coffee, OR one soda and one coffee OR two sodas.
6. 12

Page 167
1. $1.35
2. 3:57 PM; $179.30
3. $50.75
4. on a Saturday, Sunday, or holiday
5. 30 minutes
6. 18 minutes

Page 168
1. They will tie.
2. 10
3. 26.3 meters from Diane's starting spot
4. Trevor, Tristan, Tim, Troy, Tom
5. Kevin, Andrew, Malcolm, Mike, Karima, Andres

Page 169
1. 22 shots
2. 135 shots
3. 18%
4. 27.5%
5. 400 points
6. 20%

Pages 170–171
1. 14
2. 112
3. 1:9
4. 71
5. 89%
6. 16
7. games 1, 5, and 7
8. game 3
9. 19
10. 82
11. 19:82
12. 30.8%
13. game 8
14. games 5 and 8
15. 63
16. games 2 and 10

Page 172
1.

2. Marty
3.

Page 173
1. Tigers 90%
   Bears 45%
   Lions 40%
   Zebras 35%
   Giraffes 25%
2. Grace 60%
   Tristan 50%
   Maggie 25%
   Scott 30%
   Jason 36%

Page 174
1. 11
2. 86 minutes
3. 450
4. 310 minutes
5. 4
6. $\frac{2}{19}$

Page 175
1. Keisha bought 3.02 lbs of cheese and 2.8 lbs of roast beef. Samantha bought 2.37 lbs of sausage and 4.4 lbs of hot dogs. Carla bought 2.38 lbs of turkey and 2.75 lbs of ham. Allegra bought 4 lbs of potato salad and 3 lbs of macaroni salad.
3. chicken salad and egg salad
4. $1.54

Page 176
1. About 4 feet, 6 inches; to determine this, assume that the Statue of Liberty has the same dimensions of a real person, just on a larger scale. So:

$$\frac{\text{length of your nose} \times \text{length of Statue of Liberty's arm}}{\text{length of your arm}}$$

2. 32 feet
3. Answers will vary, but generally yes.
4. The larger image should look identical to the smaller image.

Page 177
1. $m = 2j + 3$ or similar
2. $t = 4(m + j)$ or similar
3. $j = 18 + m$ or similar
4. $m + w = s + t$ or similar
5. $t = (m + j) - 16$ or similar
6. $j = (m + t) - 5$ or similar
7. $m = 5j$ or similar
8. $s = t + 7$ or similar
9. $m = \frac{1}{4}t$ or similar
10. $s = 2m - 3$ or similar

Page 178
1. 10 years
2. For 2008:
   $2008 - 1924 = 84$ Years
   $\frac{84 \text{ years}}{7 \text{ years}} = 12$ doublings
   $3,000 \times 2^{12} = \$12,288,000.00$
3. Answers will vary.
4. $192.00
5. $384.00; It is better to have a shorter loan period because you will have less to pay back in the long run.

Page 179
1. correct
2. correct
3. incorrect
4. correct
5. correct
6. incorrect
7. correct
8. incorrect
9. correct
10. correct
This student's grade is 70%.

Page 180
1. Answers will vary.
2. 20
3. There are 13 stars above the eagle on the back of a one-dollar bill.

Page 181
Answers will vary slightly, depending on the person; the length of fingers does not affect the measure of the angles between the fingers.

Page 182
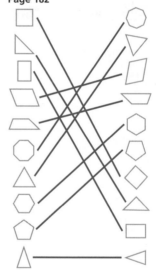

Page 183
1. the Hershstall
2. Because it gets relatively low gas mileage. If the tank was small, the driver would have to fill it up with gas very frequently. It would not be convenient.
3. the Hershstall
4. the Minitroop
5. Wednesday, the third day

Page 184
1. $2.5 \times 2.5 \times 1.4 = 8.75$
   $8.75 \times 1,000 = 8,750$
2. $1.7 \times 1.3 \times 2 = 4.42$
   $4.42 \times 1,000 = 4,42$
3. $0.7 \times 0.5 \times 0.9 = 0.315$
   $0.315 \times 1,000 = 315$
4. $1.2 \times 0.9 \times 1.2 = 1.296$
   $1.296 \times 1,000 = 1,296$
5. $1.9 \times 1.9 \times 1.9 = 6.859$
   $6.859 \times 1,000 = 6,859$
6. $1.9 \times 4.4 \times 2.4 = 20.064$
   $20.064 \times 1,000 = 20,064$
7. $4 \times 4 \times 3.3 = 52.8$
   $52.8 \times 1,000 = 52,800$
8. $3.6 \times 3.2 \times 2.3 = 26.496$
   $26.496 \times 1,000 = 26,496$

Page 185
1. C and E

A and B	20%	10%	10%	40%	15%
A and C	10%	15%	35%	30%	10%
A and D	30%	20%	20%	8%	22%
A and E	5%	2%	30%	25%	2%
B and C	30%	25%	25%	10%	25%
B and D	10%	10%	10%	32%	37%
B and E	25%	12%	20%	15%	17%
C and D	40%	35%	15%	22%	12%
C and E	5%	13%	5%	5%	8%
D and E	35%	22%	10%	17%	20%

2. 40
3. Site D
4. Site C